180 Days of
SCIENCE
for First Grade

flower

seed

leaf

stem

root

Author
Lauren Homayoun

SHELL EDUCATION

Earth & Space
Life
Physical

Publishing Credits

Corinne Burton, M.A.Ed., *Publisher*
Conni Medina, M.A.Ed., *Managing Editor*
Emily R. Smith, M.A.Ed., *Content Director*
Shaun Bernadou, *Art Director*
Lynette Ordoñez, *Editor*

Image Credits

p.116, p.117 Cherednychenko Ihor/Shutterstock; all other images from iStock and/or Shutterstock.

Standards

© 2014 Mid-continent Research for Education and Learning (McREL)
NGSS Lead States. 2013. Next Generation Science Standards: For States, By States.
Washington, DC: The National Academies Press.

For information on how this resource meets national and other state standards, see pages 10–13. You may also review this information by visiting our website at www.teachercreatedmaterials.com/administrators/correlations/ and following the on-screen directions.

Shell Education

A division of Teacher Created Materials
5301 Oceanus Drive
Huntington Beach, CA 92649-1030
www.tcmpub.com/shell-education

ISBN 978-1-4258-1407-6
©2018 Shell Educational Publishing, Inc.

Table of Contents

Introduction 3

How to Use This Book 4

Standards Correlations 9

Daily Practice Pages 14

Answer Key 194

Rubrics 202

Analysis Pages 205

Digital Resources 208

Introduction

With today's science and technology, there are more resources than ever to help students understand how the world works. Information about science experiments you can do at home is widely available online. Many students have experience with physics concepts from games.

While students may be familiar with many of the topics discussed in this book, it is not uncommon for them to have misconceptions about certain subjects. It is important for students to learn how to apply scientific practices in a classroom setting and within their lives.

Science is the study of the physical and natural world through observation and experiment. Not only is it important for students to learn scientific facts, but it is important for them to develop a thirst for knowledge. This leads to students who are anxious to learn and who understand how to follow practices that will lead them to the answers they seek.

The Need for Practice

To be successful in science, students must understand how people interact with the physical world. They must not only master scientific practices but also learn how to look at the world with curiosity. Through repeated practice, students will learn how a variety of factors affect the world in which they live.

Understanding Assessment

In addition to providing opportunities for frequent practice, teachers must be able to assess students' scientific understandings. This allows teachers to adequately address students' misconceptions, build on their current understandings, and challenge them appropriately. Assessment is a long-term process that involves careful analysis of student responses from discussions, projects, or practice sheets. The data gathered from assessments should be used to inform instruction: slow down, speed up, or reteach. This type of assessment is called *formative assessment*.

How to Use This Book

Weekly Structure

All 36 weeks of this book follow a regular weekly structure. The book is divided into three sections: Life Science, Physical Science, and Earth and Space Science. The book is structured to give students a strong foundation on which to build throughout the year. It is also designed to adequately prepare them for state standardized tests.

Each week focuses on one topic. Day 1 sets the stage by providing background information on the topic that students will need throughout the week. In Day 2, students analyze data related to the topic. Day 3 leads students through developing scientific questions. Day 4 guides students through planning a solution. Finally, Day 5 helps students communicate results from observations or investigations.

 Day 1—Learning Content: Students will read grade-appropriate content and answer questions about it.

 Day 2—Analyzing Data: Students will analyze scientific data and answer questions about it.

 Day 3—Developing Questions: Students will read a scenario related to the topic, answer questions, and formulate a scientific question about the information.

 Day 4—Planning Solutions: Students will read a scenario related to the topic, answer questions, and develop a solution or plan an investigation.

 Day 5—Communicating Results: Students accurately communicate the results of an investigation or demonstrate what they learned throughout the week.

Three Strands of Science

This book allows students to explore the three strands of science: life science, physical science, and earth and space science. Life science teaches students about the amazing living things on our planet and how they interact in ecosystems. Physical science introduces students to physics and chemistry concepts that will lay the groundwork for deeper understanding later in their education. Earth and space science familiarizes students with the wonders of the cosmos and the relationships between the sun, Earth, moon, and stars.

How to Use This Book *(cont.)*

Weekly Topics

The following chart shows the weekly focus topics that are covered during each week of instruction.

Unit	Week	Science Topic
Life Science	1	What Living Things Need
	2	What Do All Living Things Have?
	3	Parts of a Plant
	4	Parts of the Human Body
	5	Life Cycles of Plants
	6	Life Cycles of Bugs
	7	Young Animals in the Jungle
	8	How Animals Teach Their Young
	9	Similarities between Baby Animals and Their Parents
	10	Similarities between Young and Mature Plants
	11	Inherited Traits in Animals
	12	Inherited and Environmental Traits in People
Physical Science	1	How Does Sound Happen?
	2	How Animals Make Sounds
	3	How People Hear
	4	How People See
	5	Light Sources
	6	Things That Can't Be Seen
	7	Transparent, Translucent, and Opaque Objects
	8	Light Reflection
	9	Sending Messages With Sound and Light
	10	Long-Distance Communication Using Sound and Light
	11	Making Sound Travel Farther
	12	Using Light for Long-Distance Communication
Earth and Space Science	1	The Sun, Moon, and Stars
	2	Patterns of the Sun and Moon
	3	The Earth and Sun
	4	The Seasons and the Sun
	5	The Sun Appears to Move from East to West
	6	The Earth and the Moon
	7	Phases of the Moon
	8	Can People Live on the Moon?
	9	Overview of Stars and Constellations
	10	When Can You See the Stars?
	11	The Stars are Innumerable
	12	Stars Are All Different

How to Use This Book *(cont.)*

Best Practices for This Series

- Use the practice pages to introduce important science topics to your students.

- Use the Weekly Topics chart on page 5 to align the content to what you're covering in class. Then, treat the pages in this book as jumping off points for that content.

- Use the practice pages as formative assessment of the science strands and key topics.

- Use the weekly themes to engage students in content that is new to them.

- Encourage students to independently learn more about the topics introduced in this series.

- Lead teacher-directed discussions of the vocabulary and concepts presented in some of the more complex weeks.

- Support students in practicing the varied types of questions asked throughout the practice pages.

- When possible, have students participate in hands-on activities to answer the questions they generate and do the investigations they plan.

Using the Resources

An answer key for all days can be found on pages 194–201. Rubrics for Day 3 (developing questions), Day 4 (planning solutions), and Day 5 (communicating results) can be found on pages 202–204 and in the Digital Resources. Use the answer keys and rubrics to assess students' work. Be sure to share these rubrics with students so that they know what is expected of them.

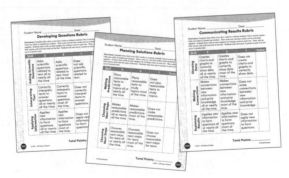

How to Use This Book *(cont.)*

Diagnostic Assessment

Teachers can use the practice pages as diagnostic assessments. The data analysis tools included with the book enable teachers or parents to quickly score students' work and monitor their progress. Teachers and parents can see which skills students may need to target further to develop proficiency.

Students will learn science content, how to analyze data, how to develop scientific questions, how to plan solutions, and how to accurately communicate results. You can assess students' learning using the answer key for all days. Rubrics are also provided on pages 202–204 for Days 3–5 to help you further assess key analytical skills that are needed for success with the scientific practices. Then, record their scores on the Practice Page Item Analysis sheets (pages 205–207). These charts are provided as PDFs, Microsoft Word® files, and Microsoft Excel® files. Teachers can input data into the electronic files directly, or they can print the pages.

To Complete the Practice Page Analysis Charts

- Write or type students' names in the far-left column. Depending on the number of students, more than one copy of the form may be needed or you may need to add rows.

  - The science strands are indicated across the tops of the charts.

  - Students should be assessed every four weeks, as indicated in the first rows of the charts.

- For each student, evaluate his or her work over the past four weeks using the answer key for Days 1 and 2 and the rubrics for Days 3–5.

- Review students' work for the weeks indicated in the chart. For example, if using the *Life Science Analysis Chart* for the first time, review students' work from weeks 1–4. Add the scores for Days 1 and 2 for each student, and record those in the appropriate columns. Then, write students' rubric scores for Days 3–5 in the corresponding columns. Use these scores as benchmarks to determine how each student is performing.

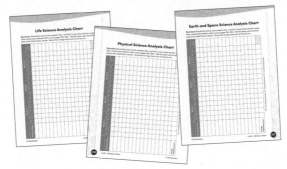

Digital Resources

The Digital Resources contain digital copies of the rubrics, analysis sheets, and standards correlations. See page 208 for more information.

How to Use This Book *(cont.)*

Using the Results to Differentiate Instruction

Once results are gathered and analyzed, teachers can use the results to inform the way they differentiate instruction. The data can help determine which science skills and topics are the most difficult for students and which students need additional instructional support and continued practice.

Whole-Class Support

The results of the diagnostic analysis may show that the entire class is struggling with certain science topics. If these concepts have been taught in the past, this indicates that further instruction or reteaching is necessary. If these concepts have not been taught in the past, this data is a great preassessment and may demonstrate that students do not have a working knowledge of the concepts. Thus, careful planning for the length of the unit(s) or lesson(s) must be considered, and additional front-loading may be required.

Small-Group or Individual Support

The results of the diagnostic analysis may show that an individual student or a small group of students is struggling with certain science skills. If these concepts have been taught in the past, this indicates that further instruction or reteaching is necessary. Consider pulling these students aside to instruct them further on the concepts while others are working independently. Students may also benefit from extra practice using games or computer-based resources.

Teachers can also use the results to help identify proficient individual students or groups of students who are ready for enrichment or above-grade-level instruction. These students may benefit from independent learning contracts or more challenging activities.

Standards Correlations

Shell Education is committed to producing educational materials that are research and standards based. In this effort, we have correlated all of our products to the academic standards of all 50 states, the District of Columbia, the Department of Defense Dependents Schools, and all Canadian provinces.

How to Find Standards Correlations

To print a customized correlation report of this product for your state, visit our website at **www.teachercreatedmaterials.com/administrators/correlations/** and follow the on-screen directions. If you require assistance in printing correlation reports, please contact our Customer Service Department at 1-877-777-3450.

Purpose and Intent of Standards

The Every Student Succeeds Act (ESSA) mandates that all states adopt challenging academic standards that help students meet the goal of college and career readiness. While many states already adopted academic standards prior to ESSA, the act continues to hold states accountable for detailed and comprehensive standards.

Standards are designed to focus instruction and guide adoption of curricula. Standards are statements that describe the criteria necessary for students to meet specific academic goals. They define the knowledge, skills, and content students should acquire at each level. Standards are also used to develop standardized tests to evaluate students' academic progress. Teachers are required to demonstrate how their lessons meet state standards. State standards are used in the development of all of our products, so educators can be assured they meet the academic requirements of each state.

McREL Compendium

Each year, McREL analyzes state standards and revises the compendium to produce a general compilation of national standards. The standards listed on page 10 support the objectives presented throughout the weeks.

Next Generation Science Standards

This set of national standards aims to incorporate knowledge and process standards into a cohesive framework. The standards listed on pages 10–13 support the objectives presented throughout the weeks.

Standards Correlations *(cont.)*

180 Days of Science is designed to give students daily practice in the three strands of science. The weeks support the McREL standards and NGSS performance expectations listed in the charts below.

McREL Standards		
Standard	**Weeks**	**Unit**
Knows that plants and animals need certain resources for energy and growth.	1	Life Science
Knows that plants and animals have features that help them live in different environments.	1–7	Life Science
Understands that living things have similar needs.	2	Life Science
Knows that plants and animals closely resemble their parents.	9, 10	Life Science
Knows that differences exist among individuals of the same kind of plant or animal.	11, 12	Life Science
Knows that things can vibrate.	1–3	Physical Science
Knows that sound is produced by vibrating objects.	1–3	Physical Science
Knows that light travels in a straight line until it hits an object.	7, 8	Physical Science
Knows basic patterns of the sun and moon.	2–5, 7, 8	Earth and Space Science
Knows that the stars are innumerable, unevenly dispersed, and of unequal brightness.	9–12	Earth and Space Science

Next Generation Science Standards					
Unit	**Week**	**Performance Expectation**	**Science and Engineering Practices**	**Disciplinary Core Ideas**	**Cross-Cutting Concepts**
Life Science	1	Use materials to design a solution to a human problem by mimicking how plants and/or animals use their external parts to help them survive, grow, and meet their needs.	Obtaining, Evaluating, and Communicating Information	Information Processing	Structure and Function
	2	Use materials to design a solution to a human problem by mimicking how plants and/or animals use their external parts to help them survive, grow, and meet their needs.	Constructing Explanations and Designing Solutions	Structure and Function	Patterns Structure and Function Influence of Engineering, Technology, and Science, on Society and the Natural World
	3	Use materials to design a solution to a human problem by mimicking how plants and/or animals use their external parts to help them survive, grow, and meet their needs.	Obtaining, Evaluating, and Communicating Information	Structure and Function	Structure and Function
	4	Use materials to design a solution to a human problem by mimicking how plants and/or animals use their external parts to help them survive, grow, and meet their needs.	Obtaining, Evaluating, and Communicating Information	Structure and Function	Structure and Function

Standards Correlations *(cont.)*

Unit	Week	Performance Expectation	Science and Engineering Practices	Disciplinary Core Ideas	Cross-Cutting Concepts
Life Science	5	Read texts and use media to determine patterns in behavior of parents and offspring that help offspring survive.	Obtaining, Evaluating, and Communicating Information	Growth and Development of Organisms Information Processing	Patterns
	6	Read texts and use media to determine patterns in behavior of parents and offspring that help offspring survive.	Obtaining, Evaluating, and Communicating Information	Growth and Development of Organisms	Patterns
	7	Read texts and use media to determine patterns in behavior of parents and offspring that help offspring survive.	Obtaining, Evaluating, and Communicating Information	Growth and Development of Organisms	Patterns
	8	Read texts and use media to determine patterns in behavior of parents and offspring that help offspring survive.	Obtaining, Evaluating, and Communicating Information	Growth and Development of Organisms	Patterns
	9	Make observations to construct an evidence-based account that young plants and animals are like, but not exactly like, their parents.	Constructing Explanations and Designing Solutions Obtaining, Evaluating, and Communicating Information	Variation of Traits	Patterns
	10	Make observations to construct an evidence-based account that young plants and animals are like, but not exactly like, their parents.	Obtaining, Evaluating, and Communicating Information	Variation of Traits	Patterns
	11	Make observations to construct an evidence-based account that young plants and animals are like, but not exactly like, their parents.	Constructing Explanations and Designing Solutions Obtaining, Evaluating, and Communicating Information	Inheritance of Traits Variation of Traits	Patterns
	12	Make observations to construct an evidence-based account that young plants and animals are like, but not exactly like, their parents.	Constructing Explanations and Designing Solutions Obtaining, Evaluating, and Communicating Information	Inheritance of Traits Variation of Traits	Patterns
Physical Science	1	Plan and conduct investigations to provide evidence that vibrating materials can make sound and that sound can make materials vibrate.	Planning and Carrying Out Investigations Constructing Explanations and Designing Solutions	Wave Properties	Cause and Effect

Next Generation Science Standards

Standards Correlations *(cont.)*

Unit	Week	Performance Expectation	Science and Engineering Practices	Disciplinary Core Ideas	Cross-Cutting Concepts
		Next Generation Science Standards			
Physical Science	2	Plan and conduct investigations to provide evidence that vibrating materials can make sound and that sound can make materials vibrate.	Constructing Explanations and Designing Solutions	Wave Properties	Cause and Effect
	3	Plan and conduct investigations to provide evidence that vibrating materials can make sound and that sound can make materials vibrate.	Planning and Carrying Out Investigations	Wave Properties	Cause and Effect
	4	Make observations to construct an evidence-based account that objects can be seen only when illuminated.	Planning and Carrying Out Investigations Constructing Explanations and Designing Solutions	Electromagnetic Radiation	Cause and Effect Influence of Engineering, Technology, and Science, on Society and the Natural World
	5	Make observations to construct an evidence-based account that objects can be seen only when illuminated.	Constructing Explanations and Designing Solutions	Electromagnetic Radiation	Cause and Effect
	6	Make observations to construct an evidence-based account that objects can be seen only when illuminated.	Constructing Explanations and Designing Solutions	Electromagnetic Radiation	Cause and Effect Influence of Engineering, Technology, and Science, on Society and the Natural World
	7	Plan and conduct an investigation to determine the effect of placing objects made with different materials in the path of a beam of light.	Planning and Carrying Out Investigations	Electromagnetic Radiation	Cause and Effect
	8	Plan and conduct an investigation to determine the effect of placing objects made with different materials in the path of a beam of light.	Planning and Carrying Out Investigations	Electromagnetic Radiation	Cause and Effect
	9	Use tools and materials to design and build a device that uses light or sound to solve the problem of communicating over a distance.	Constructing Explanations and Designing Solutions	Information Technologies and Instrumentation	Cause and Effect Influence of Engineering, Technology, and Science, on Society and the Natural World
	10	Use tools and materials to design and build a device that uses light or sound to solve the problem of communicating over a distance.	Constructing Explanations and Designing Solutions Planning and Carrying Out Investigations	Information Technologies and Instrumentation	Cause and Effect Influence of Engineering, Technology, and Science, on Society and the Natural World
	11	Use tools and materials to design and build a device that uses light or sound to solve the problem of communicating over a distance.	Planning and Carrying Out Investigations	Information Technologies and Instrumentation	Cause and Effect Influence of Engineering, Technology, and Science, on Society and the Natural World

Standards Correlations *(cont.)*

Unit	Week	Performance Expectation	Science and Engineering Practices	Disciplinary Core Ideas	Cross-Cutting Concepts
Next Generation Science Standards					
Physical Science	12	Use tools and materials to design and build a device that uses light or sound to solve the problem of communicating over a distance.	Planning and Carrying Out Investigations	Information Technologies and Instrumentation	Cause and Effect Influence of Engineering, Technology, and Science, on Society and the Natural World
Earth and Space Science	1	Use observations of the sun, moon, and stars to describe patterns that can be predicted.	Analyzing and Interpreting Data	The Universe and Its Stars	Patterns Scientific Knowledge Assumes an Order and Consistency in Natural Systems
	2	Use observations of the sun, moon, and stars to describe patterns that can be predicted.	Planning and Carrying Out Investigations	The Universe and Its Stars	Patterns
	3	Use observations of the sun, moon, and stars to describe patterns that can be predicted.	Analyzing and Interpreting Data	The Universe and Its Stars	Patterns
	4	Make observations at different times of year to relate the amount of daylight to the time of year.	Analyzing and Interpreting Data	Earth and the Solar System	Patterns Scientific Knowledge Assumes an Order and Consistency in Natural Systems
	5	Use observations of the sun, moon, and stars to describe patterns that can be predicted.	Analyzing and Interpreting Data	The Universe and Its Stars Earth and the Solar System	Patterns Scientific Knowledge Assumes an Order and Consistency in Natural Systems
	6	Use observations of the sun, moon, and stars to describe patterns that can be predicted.	Analyzing and Interpreting Data	Earth and the Solar System	Patterns
	7	Use observations of the sun, moon, and stars to describe patterns that can be predicted.	Analyzing and Interpreting Data	The Universe and Its Stars	Patterns
	8	Use observations of the sun, moon, and stars to describe patterns that can be predicted.	Analyzing and Interpreting Data	The Universe and Its Stars	Patterns
	9	Use observations of the sun, moon, and stars to describe patterns that can be predicted.	Planning and Carrying Out Investigations	The Universe and Its Stars	Patterns
	10	Use observations of the sun, moon, and stars to describe patterns that can be predicted.	Analyzing and Interpreting Data	The Universe and Its Stars	Patterns
	11	Use observations of the sun, moon, and stars to describe patterns that can be predicted.	Analyzing and Interpreting Data	The Universe and Its Stars	Patterns
	12	Use observations of the sun, moon, and stars to describe patterns that can be predicted.	Analyzing and Interpreting Data	The Universe and Its Stars	Patterns

Name: _____ **Date:** _____

Directions: Read the text. Answer the questions.

What Living Things Need

Plants are alive. Animals are alive. They are both living things. Plants need light and water to live and grow. Animals need food to live and grow. They need water, too. Some things aren't alive. They don't need food or water.

1. Plants need _____ to live and grow.

   a. light and food   **b.** light and water

   c. food and water   **d.** water and animals

2. All living things need _____ .

   a. water   **b.** sleep

   c. food   **d.** light

Name: _____ **Date:** _____

Directions: Look at the chart about living and non-living things. Answer the questions.

Analyzing Data

	Living	Non-Living
Does it grow?	✔ Yes	✗ No
Does it need food?	✔ Yes	✗ No
Does it need water?	✔ Yes	✗ No

1. Do all living things grow?

   a. yes

   b. no

2. Do non-living things need water?

   a. yes

   b. no

3. Do living things need food?

   a. yes

   b. no

Name: _____ **Date:** _____

Directions: Read the text. Answer the questions.

Developing Questions

Maria has a plant. It is in a sunny window. She asks her brother to water it. She looks at it two days later. The plant looks bad. Its leaves are brown. Maria thinks her brother forgot to water it.

1. What makes Maria think her brother forgot to water her plant?

   a. The leaves are brown.

   b. The plant isn't in the window anymore.

   c. The plant looks good.

   d. The leaves are green.

2. What is a question that Maria could ask about her plant?

   _____

   _____

   _____

   _____

Name: _____ Date: _____

Directions: Read the text. Answer the questions.

Dylan has a new cat. She doesn't know what kind of food her new cat likes. She gets three different cans of food for her cat. One kind of food is made of chicken. Another kind of food is made of fish. The third kind of food is made of rice.

1. How can Dylan test which food her cat likes best?

   a. She can put the food in three bowls.

   b. She can give one food.

   c. She can give two foods.

   d. She can put all the food in the same bowl.

2. Should Dylan give her cat the different types of food at the same time or at different times? Why?

   _____

   _____

   _____

   _____

Communicating Results

Name: _____ Date: _____

Directions: Read the text. Answer the questions.

Dylan has a new cat. She wants to know what kind of food her cat likes best. She puts her cat's food in three bowls. Her cat doesn't eat any of the food made of rice. He eats half of the food made of chicken. He eats all of the food made of fish.

1. Color the amount of food Dylan's cat eats in each bowl.

Rice   **Chicken**   **Fish**

 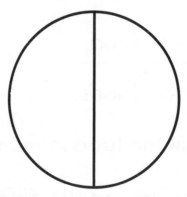 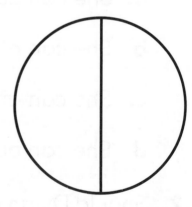

2. Which food does the cat like best? How can you tell?

_____

_____

_____

_____

Name: _____ **Date:** _____

Directions: Read the text. Answer the questions.

What Do All Living Things Have?

All living things have parts. Plants have different parts. These parts help them grow. Animals have different parts, too. Animals use their body parts to get food. They use their parts to protect themselves. They use their body parts to move. All living things have the parts they need.

1. _____ have different parts.

   a. Only animals

   b. Plants and animals

   c. Only plants

   d. Neither plants nor animals

2. Animals have _____ the parts they need to live in their homes.

   a. all of

   b. most of

   c. none of

   d. two of

Learning Content

Analyzing Data

Name: _____ **Date:** _____

Directions: Read the names of the parts of a duck. Answer the questions.

eye

wing

beak

tail

feet

1. What part of a duck helps it fly?

    a. wings   **b.** beak

    c. eye   **d.** feet

2. What part does a duck use to walk?

    a. beak   **b.** feet

    c. wing   **d.** tail

51407—180 Days of Science

Name: _____   Date: _____

Directions: Look at the pictures. Read the text.
Answer the questions.

> Some animals have shells. Shells help protect
> them. You have a bike helmet. It helps protect you.

Developing Questions

1. How is a bike helmet like a turtle shell?

    a. They are the same shape.

    b. They are the same color.

    c. They are both striped.

    d. They are both smooth.

2. What could you ask about the helmet's shape?

_____

_____

_____

_____

Planning Solutions

Name: _____ **Date:** _____

Directions: Read the text. Look at the pictures. Then, answer the questions.

> Some plants have sharp parts. Sharp parts help protect the plant. Some animals have sharp parts, too. These help protect the animal.
>
>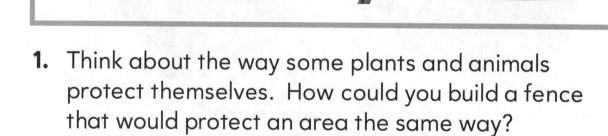

1. Think about the way some plants and animals protect themselves. How could you build a fence that would protect an area the same way?

   a. Give the fence sharp parts.

   b. Give the fence soft parts.

   c. Give the fence sticky parts.

2. You see a rose. It has many thorns. Why can this be a problem?

   _____

   _

   _____

   _

   _____

Name: _____ **Date:** _____

ABC

Directions: Read the text. Put an X in the correct boxes of the chart. Then, answer the question.

> Birds that swim a lot have special feet. Their feet are webbed. This means their toes are connected.

Communicating Results

	Duck	Sparrow	Penguin
Webbed feet			
Not webbed feet			

1. Why might birds that swim a lot have webbed feet?

_____

_ _

_ _

_ _

_____

Learning Content

Name: _____ **Date:** _____

Directions: Read the text, and look at the picture. Answer the questions.

Parts of Plants

Plants have different parts that help them live and grow. Leaves soak up sunlight. The sunlight gives plants get their energy. They use this energy to grow. Stems and trunks hold plants up. Roots soak up water. Plants need water to live. Some plants have flowers that make seeds. If the plants get the right amount of water and sun, new plants grow from the seeds.

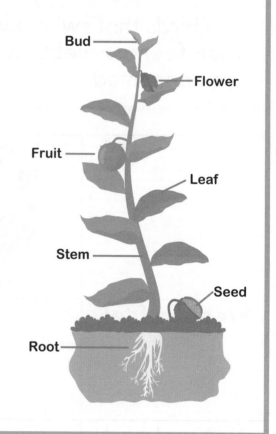

1. What part of a plant soaks up water?

   a. leaves   **b.** roots

   c. bud   **d.** fruit

2. Would a plant grow if it did not get any sun?

   a. yes   **b.** no

Name: _____ **Date:** _____

Directions: Sam tested to see how much water a type of plant needs. Look at his chart. Then answer the questions.

	Plant 1	Plant 2
Water given each week	2 cups of water	1 cup of water
Week 1 growth	3 inches	2 inches
Week 2 growth	4 inches	1 inch

1. Which plant grew the most?

   a. plant 1   **b.** plant 2

   c. neither   **d.** both

2. How much water is best for this type of plant?

   a. 1 cup each week   **b.** 2 cups each week

   c. less than 1 cup   **d.** more than 2 cups

Analyzing Data

Developing Questions

Name: _____ **Date:** _____

Directions: Read the text. Answer the questions.

Lisa helped her mom grow a garden. Lisa visits her garden. The plants do not all look the same. On one side of the garden, the plants' leaves are turning brown. On the other side, the leaves are green.

1. What part of the plants did Lisa look at?

   a. leaves   **b.** flowers

   c. fruit   **d.** stems

2. What is the difference between the two sides of the garden?

   _____

   _ _ _ _ _ _ _ _ _ _ _ _ _ _ _ _ _

   _____

   _____

   _ _ _ _ _ _ _ _ _ _ _ _ _ _ _ _ _

   _____

3. Tell a friend a question Lisa might ask about her garden.

51407—180 Days of Science   © *Shell Education*

Name: _____ Date: _____

Directions: Read the text. Answer the questions.

On one side of Lisa's garden, the leaves are turning brown. The leaves on the other side are still green. Lisa wants to know why some plants are brown.

1. Which plants have what they need to live and grow?

   a. the green plants

   b. the brown plants

   c. both plants

   d. neither plant

2. What could Lisa do to find out what is making the plants brown?

   _____

   _

   _____

   _

   _____

Name: _____ **Date:** _____

Directions: Read Lisa's notes about her garden. Fill in the chart. Answer the question.

> The plants on the left side of the garden are brown. The plants on the right side are green. Both sides of the garden get bright sunlight all day long. The plants on the right side get lots of water. The plants on the left get a little water.

	Plants on the Left	**Plants on the Right**
plant color		
amount of sunlight		
amount of water		

1. Should Lisa try giving the plants on the left more water or more sun? Why?

_____

_ _

_____

_ _

_____

Communicating Results

Name: _____   Date: _____

Directions: Read the text. Answer the questions.

The Human Body

You have a body. Your body has parts. Some parts are big, like your legs and your back. Some parts are smaller. Some of the smaller parts are your eyes, ears, hands, nose, and mouth. You use these parts to see, hear, touch, smell, and taste.

1. Which of these is smallest?

   a. eye   **b.** hand

   c. back   **d.** leg

2. Which of these is biggest?

   a. nose   **b.** legs

   c. eyes   **d.** mouth

Name: _____ **Date:** _____

Directions: Study the chart. Answer the questions.

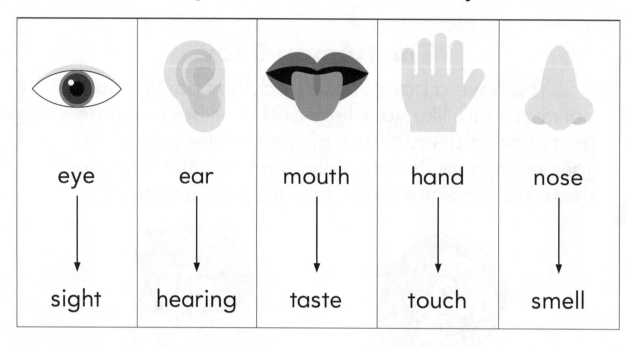

eye	ear	mouth	hand	nose
↓	↓	↓	↓	↓
sight	hearing	taste	touch	smell

1. Which body part helps you taste a carrot?

   a. nose

   b. mouth

   c. ear

   d. eye

2. I use my _____ to watch TV.

   a. mouth

   b. eyes

   c. hand

   d. nose

Name: _____ **Date:** _____

Directions: Read the text. Answer the questions.

> Angela just came home from school. She puts down her backpack and walks to the kitchen. She smells something good. It smells sweet. She wonders what treat her mom baked.
>
>

1. What body part does Angela use to walk into the kitchen?

   a. feet   **b.** hands

   c. mouth   **d.** ears

2. What is something you'd like to ask about how Angela knew her mom baked a treat?

   _____

   _____

   _____

   _____

   _____

   _____

Planning Solutions

Name: _____ Date: _____

Directions: Read the text. Answer the questions.

It's a snowy day! Jay brings his brother, Micah, and his sister, Missy, some hot chocolate. Micah and Missy see the steam. They feel the hot cup. They know the chocolate is too hot to drink.

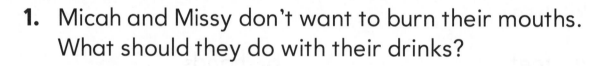

1. Micah and Missy don't want to burn their mouths. What should they do with their drinks?

   a. Wait until they cool off.

   b. Use a straw.

   c. Drink them fast.

   d. Drink them slowly.

2. How could they cool their drinks off faster?

   _____

   _____

   _____

   _____

Name: _____ **Date:** _____

Directions: Look at the chart. Then, draw a picture of a person. Make sure you draw the right number of body parts.

How many parts do people have?	
Eyes	2
Ears	2
Nose	1
Hands	2
Mouth	1
Legs	2

Learning Content

Name: _____ Date: _____

Directions: Read the text. Answer the questions.

Young Plants

Most plants start as seeds. Seeds have hard coverings. They are called seed coats. As the seeds grow, the seed coats break. Then roots grow. Next, little sprouts come out of the top of the seeds. The plants pop out of the ground. The baby plants then become seedlings. The seedlings grow leaves. They will soon be grown-up plants.

1. The covering on the outside of a seed is called a
   _____ .

   a. leaf   **b.** seed coat

   c. root   **d.** sprout

2. Which grows first?

   a. roots   **b.** leaves

   c. sprouts   **d.** seedlings

Name: _____ **Date:** _____

Directions: Read the text. Study the chart. Answer the questions.

> Plants take time to come out of the ground. This is called germination.

Plant	Days to Germination
carrot	6
lettuce	3
parsley	14
tomato	6
cucumber	10

1. Which plant germinates the most quickly?

   a. tomato   **b.** lettuce

   c. carrot   **d.** cucumber

2. Which plant takes the longest time to germinate?

   a. parsley   **b.** carrot

   c. tomato   **d.** cucumber

Name: _____ **Date:** _____

Directions: Read the text. Answer the questions.

Sprouts grow out of the tops of seeds. They often look alike. When plants get bigger, they grow leaves. Leaves come in many shapes and sizes. Scientists use leaves to tell plants apart.

1. A scientist sees a sprout. Can the scientist tell what kind of plant is growing?

    a. Yes, because all sprouts are different.

    b. No, because sprouts often look alike.

2. What is a question the scientist might ask about the sprout?

    _____

    _

    _____

    _

    _____

Name: _____ **Date:** _____

Directions: Read the text. Answer the questions.

> Some seeds are big. Some seeds are small. Some big plants grow from small seeds. Some small plants grow from big seeds. You can't always tell how big a grown-up plant will be by looking at its seed. You have to find out how big the grown-up plant will be.

1. If the seed is small, will the plant always be small?

  a. yes

  b. no

2. How can you find out how big a grown-up plant will be?

_____

- -

_____

_____

- -

_____

Name: _____ **Date:** _____

Directions: Number the boxes in the order a plant grows. Then, draw a picture of a flower in the empty box.

	Sprout		Seedling

	Seed with root		Seed

	Grown-up plant	6	Flower

Learning Content

Name: _____ **Date:** _____

Directions: Read the text. Answer the questions.

Young Bugs

Most bugs start as eggs. Bugs lay many eggs at once. They lay eggs in areas that are safe and have a lot of food. When the eggs hatch, larvae come out. Larvae do not look like adult bugs. The larvae eat a lot and grow quickly into pupae. Pupae do not eat or move around much. Pupae grow and become adult bugs.

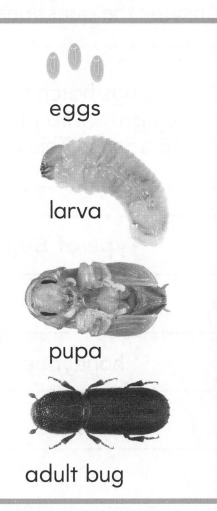

eggs

larva

pupa

adult bug

1. When eggs hatch, what comes out?

    a. pupae   **b.** larvae

    c. adult bugs   **d.** young bugs

2. How can you tell that a bug is a larva?

    a. It looks like an egg.   **b.** It doesn't eat much.

    c. It doesn't move   **d.** It looks different
        around much.   from an adult bug.

Analyzing Data

Name: _____ **Date:** _____

Directions: Read the text. Study the chart. Answer the questions.

Bugs hatch from eggs as larvae. Then they grow into pupae. Then they grow into adults. This is called metamorphosis.

Type of Bug	Length of Metamorphosis
butterfly	30 days
honeybee	21 days
ladybug	35 days
mosquito	14 days

1. Which bug grows most quickly?

   a. honeybee   **b.** ladybug

   c. mosquito   **d.** butterfly

2. Which bug takes the longest time to grow?

   a. mosquito   **b.** honeybee

   c. ladybug   **d.** butterfly

Name: _____ Date: _____

Directions: Read the text. Answer the questions.

Jeff found a ladybug laying eggs on a leaf. The leaf was in a safe place. The next week, Jeff saw that the eggs hatched into larvae.

1. What were the bugs that hatched from the eggs called?

   a. pupae

   b. larvae

   c. eggs

   d. adults

2. What could Jeff ask about the leaf with the eggs?

   _____

   _____

   _____

   _____

   _____

Planning Solutions

Name: _____ **Date:** _____

Directions: Read the text. Answer the questions.

Jeff found a ladybug laying eggs on a leaf. The leaf was in a safe place. The next week, Jeff saw that the eggs hatched into larvae. Later, he sees lots of ladybugs.

1. What did the larvae do?

   a. flew away

   b. grew into ladybugs

   c. crawled away

   d. grew into bees

2. Should Jeff use photos or drawings to track the ladybug life cycle? Why?

   _____

   _

   _____

   _____

   _

   _____

   _____

Name: _____ Date: _____

Directions: Label the stages of a bee's life. Use the words in the box. Answer the question.

| pupa | egg | adult | larva |

Honeybee Lifecycle

_____ _____ _____ _____

1. What are some things the bee might do once it is an adult?

_____

- -

_____

_____

- -

_____

_____

- -

_____

Communicating Results

Learning Content

Name: _____ Date: _____

Directions: Read the text. Answer the questions.

Growing Up in the Jungle

Jungles are a type of forest. They have many plants. They are thick and hard to walk through. Jungles also have lots of animals. There are leopards and monkeys. There are snakes, lizards, and frogs. They all have special ways to keep themselves safe. Some blend in with plants. Some live high in the trees. Some are poisonous.

1. What is a jungle?

   a. a forest   **b.** a desert

   c. an ocean   **d.** a prairie

2. Which animal does not live in the jungle?

   a. leopard   **b.** monkey

   c. whale   **d.** frog

Name: _____ Date: _____

Directions: Study the chart. Answer the questions.

Analyzing Data

Type of Animal	What Helps It Survive
chameleon	blends in
monkey	lives in the trees
frog	bright colors
sloth	lives in the trees

1. Which two animals survive by living in the trees?

   a. chameleon and frog   **b.** monkey and sloth

   c. sloth and frog   **d.** monkey and
                                                    chameleon

2. Which animal blends in?

   a. chameleon   **b.** sloth

   c. frog   **d.** monkey

Name: _____ **Date:** _____

Directions: Read the text. Answer the questions.

Young chimps learn from watching their moms. They learn things like which foods are safe to eat and where food can be found. A young chimp sees his mom pick up  two pieces of fruit. She puts one down and gives the other piece of fruit to the young chimp.

1. What is the young chimp doing when he watches his mom?

   a. learning   **b.** playing

   c. hiding   **d.** sleeping

2. What is a question you might ask about the mom?

   _____

   _____

   _____

   _____

   _____

Name: _____ Date: _____

Directions: Read the text. Answer the questions.

Young chimps learn from watching their moms. They learn things like which foods are safe to eat and where food can be found. A young chimp sees his mom pick up two pieces of fruit. She puts one down and gives the other piece of fruit to the young chimp.

1. What might the mother chimp be teaching her young?

   a. how to groom

   b. how to use tools

   c. how to make a nest

   d. how to choose ripe fruit

2. How can you learn what types of things chimps teach their young?

   _____

   _

   _____

   _____

   _

   _____

Name: ______________________ Date: ____________

Directions: Draw a young chimp learning something from his mom. Then, answer the question.

Communicating Results

1. How will watching his mom help the young chimp grow up?

Name: _____ **Date:** _____

Directions: Read the text. Answer the questions.

What Do the Grown-ups Do?

You spend a lot of time with grown-ups. They take care of you. They teach you and play with you. They keep you safe. Many animals are left alone when they are born. There are also animals that help their young grow up. Cheetahs spend years teaching their young and keeping them safe.

1. What is something that adult animals do for their young?

   a. teach them   **b.** sing to them

   c. buy them toys   **d.** make them clothes

2. What is something that an adult animal could teach its young?

   a. how to sing a song   **b.** how to jump rope

   c. how to find food   **d.** how to dance

Learning Content

Analyzing Data

Name: _____ **Date:** _____

Directions: Study the chart. Answer the questions.

Type of Animal	How Long They Stay with Their Mothers
elephant	16 years
alligator	2 years
polar bear	$2\frac{1}{2}$ years
koala	6 months

1. Which baby stays with its mom the longest?

   a. koala   **b.** alligator

   c. polar bear   **d.** elephant

2. Which baby leaves its mom the soonest?

   a. elephant   **b.** alligator

   c. polar bear   **d.** koala

Name: _____ **Date:** _____

Directions: Read the text. Answer the questions.

Polar bear moms stay with their babies for about 2½ years. Baby polar bears are called cubs. The moms protect their cubs. They also teach them how to live.

1. What do the polar bear moms do for their cubs?

   a. Teach them how to live.

   b. Take them on trips.

   c. Show them how to play ball.

   d. Remind them to eat lunch.

2. What is a question you might ask about the polar bear mother?

   _____

   _____

   _____

   _____

Planning Solutions

Name: _____ **Date:** _____

Directions: Read the text. Answer the questions.

Polar bear moms stay with their cubs for about $2\frac{1}{2}$ years. The moms protect their cubs. They teach them how to live and hunt. You want to know how the mother teaches her cubs these things.

1. What is one way you could figure out how the mother teachers her cubs?

    a. Observe the mother and cub.

    b. Ignore the mother and cub.

    c. Ask the mother what she is doing.

2. What might the polar bear mom do to see if her cubs are learning?

    _____

    _ _ _ _ _ _ _ _ _ _ _ _ _ _ _ _ _ _

    _____

    _ _ _ _ _ _ _ _ _ _ _ _ _ _ _ _ _ _

    _____

Name: _____ **Date:** _____

Directions: Read the text. Answer the questions.

You see a polar bear mom and her cub at the zoo. The cub stays close to the mom. The cub watches everything the mom does.

Communicating Results

1. Why do you think the cub is watching the mom closely?

_____

- -

_____

_____

- -

_____

2. Draw a picture of a mother polar bear teaching her cub something.

Name: _____ **Date:** _____

Directions: Read the text. Answer the questions.

Spot the Difference

Baby animals look a lot like their parents. There are some differences, though. Chicks are small and fuzzy. Hens are larger and have smooth feathers. Baby deer have spots on their backs. Adult deer do not.

1. How do baby animals compare to adult animals?

   a. the same

   b. similar

   c. completely different

   d. different animals

2. How are kittens different from cats?

   a. smaller

   b. bigger

   c. longer tail

   d. bigger paws

Name: _____ **Date:** _____

Directions: Study the pictures. Answer the questions.

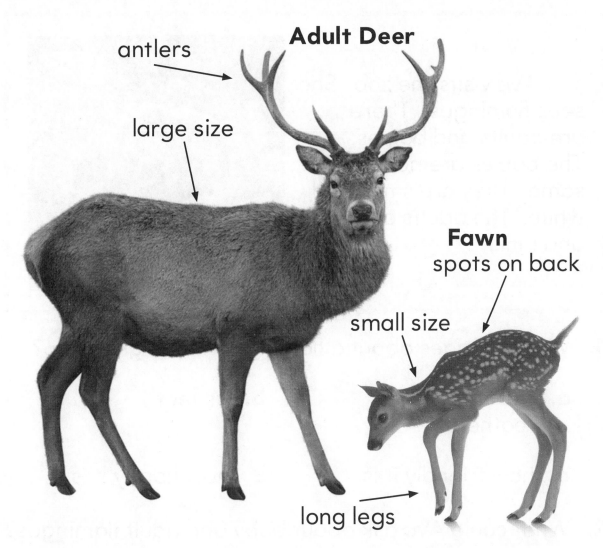

Adult Deer

antlers

large size

Fawn
spots on back

small size

long legs

1. What does the adult have that the fawn does not?

   a. fur

   b. spots

   c. antlers

   d. tail

2. What does the fawn have that the adult does not?

   a. spots

   b. hooves

   c. tail

   d. antlers

Developing Questions

Name: _____ Date: _____

Directions: Read the text. Answer the questions.

Ava visits the zoo. She sees flamingos. There are adults and babies. The babies are not the same. They are small and white. The adults are large and pink.

1. What changes about a flamingo when it grows up?

   a. the color of its feathers

   b. its feet

   c. how friendly it is

   d. how happy it is

2. What could Ava ask about baby and adult flamingos?

   _____

   _

   _____

   _

   _____

   _

   _____

51407—180 Days of Science

Planning Solutions

Name: _____ **Date:** _____

Directions: Read the text. Answer the questions.

Ava visits the zoo. She sees flamingos. The babies are white, small, and fuzzy. The adults are tall, pink, and smooth. They both have long legs. She wants to know why the adults are a different color.

1. What is one clue that the baby flamingo will look like the adult when it grows up?

   a. It is fuzzy.   **b.** It is white.

   c. It has similar legs. **d.** It is small.

2. What can Ava do to find out why the adult flamingos are pink?

   _____

   _____

   _____

   _____

Name: _____ **Date:** _____

Directions: Look at the pictures. Match the baby animals to the parents. Draw lines to connect them.

cub  • •  bear

pinky  • •  cat

fawn  • •  bull

calf  • •  mouse

chick  • •  deer

kitten  • •  rooster

Name: _____ **Date:** _____

Directions: Read the text. Answer the questions.

Almost, but Not Exactly!

Plants begin as seeds. Then they grow into seedlings. Seedlings are a little like full-grown plants. They are smaller. They do not have flowers. They have fewer leaves.

1. What may be the same between the seedling and the full-grown plant?

   a. size

   b. number of leaves

   c. leaf shape

   d. plant shape

2. How many flowers do seedlings have?

   a. 1

   b. 0

   c. 5

   d. 7

Analyzing Data

Name: _____ Date: _____

Directions: Study the picture. Answer the questions.

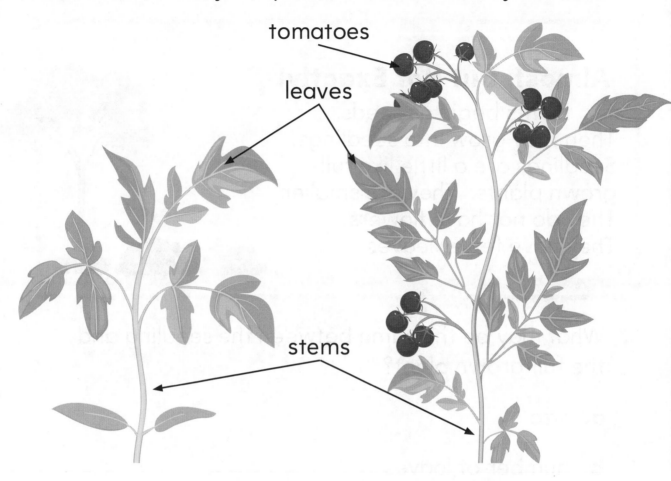

tomatoes

leaves

stems

1. What is the same between the two plants?

   a. shape of most leaves   **b.** size of the plant

   c. number of leaves   **d.** number of tomatoes

2. What is different between the two plants?

   a. shape of the leaves   **b.** amount of fruit

   c. type of stem   **d.** the type of plant

Name: _____ Date: _____

Directions: Read the text. Answer the questions.

Jose and his mother have a garden. They are growing peas and tomatoes. They are going to plant more. Jose takes pictures of the full-grown plants. He wants to compare these pictures to the new plants that grow.

1. What will Jose see when the seeds grow into seedlings?

   a. They will look exactly the same.

   b. They will look completely different.

   c. They will look alike but not exactly the same.

   d. They will be a new type of plant.

2. What might Jose ask about the new plants?

   _____

   _____

   _____

   _____

   _____

Planning Solutions

Name: _____ **Date:** _____

Directions: Read the text. Answer the questions.

Jose and his mom have a garden with peas and tomatoes. They planted some more seeds. Jose took pictures of the full-grown plants. He compared them to the new seedlings. Jose has a journal to keep track of the seedlings as they grow.

1. Will the seedlings look exactly like the full-grown plants when they are grown?

   a. yes   **b.** no

2. What can Jose track in his journal to compare the plants?

   _____

   - - - - - - - - - - - - - - - -

   _____

   - - - - - - - - - - - - - - - -

   _____

   - - - - - - - - - - - - - - - -

Name: _____ **Date:** _____

Directions: Look at the pictures. Circle the differences. Answer the question.

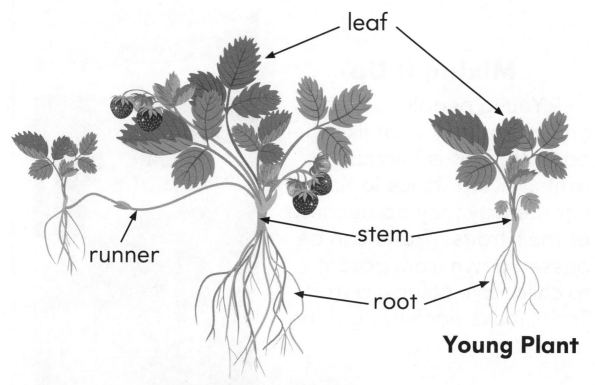

leaf

runner

stem

root

Young Plant

Full-Grown Plant

1. What will the young plant have when it is fully grown?

_____

- -

_____

_____

- -

_____

_____

- -

_____

Learning Content

Name: _____ Date: _____

Directions: Read the text. Answer the questions.

Mixing It Up

Young people, animals, and plants look a lot like their parents. This is because of traits. Living things look and act the way they do because of their traits. Traits can be passed down from parent to child. Eye color is a trait. Traits make each living thing unique.

1. What is a trait?

   a. what type of car a person drives

   b. what type of house an animal has

   c. the type of food a living thing eats

   d. how a living thing looks and behaves

2. What is an example of a trait?

   a. eye color

   b. shirt color

   c. hat color

   d. collar color

51407—180 Days of Science

Name: _____ **Date:** _____

Directions: Read the text. Study the pictures. Answer the questions.

> A puggle is a cross between a pug and a beagle. This dog shows how traits can be passed down. A puggle has traits from both the pug and the beagle.
>
>
>
> pug   puggle   beagle

1. What is one trait that the puggle shares with the beagle?

    a. flat nose   **b.** back markings

    c. floppy ears   **d.** curled tail

2. What is one trait that the puggle shares with the pug?

    a. curly fur   **b.** dark snout

    c. pointy ears   **d.** straight tail

Analyzing Data

Developing Questions

Name: _____ **Date:** _____

Directions: Read the text. Answer the questions.

Kamala's dog, Ginger, had puppies. Ginger has brown fur. The dad has yellow fur. Two of the puppies have brown fur. One puppy has yellow fur.

1. What is a reason that one of the puppies could have yellow fur?

   a. The puppy's fur hasn't turned brown yet.

   b. Ginger wished for a puppy with yellow fur.

   c. The puppy's father has yellow fur.

   d. The puppy with yellow fur isn't related.

2. What could Kamala ask about the way the puppies look?

   _____

   _____

   _____

   _____

Name: _____ **Date:** _____

Directions: Read the text. Answer the questions.

Kamala's grandma breeds dogs. Kamala loves seeing her dogs. She sees a puppy she likes. It has blue eyes. The puppy's mom does, too.

1. Where did the puppy get its blue eyes?

   a. its mom

   b. its sister

   c. Kamala

   d. the grandma

2. What can Kamala look at to see how else the puppy looks like its mom?

   _____

   _ _ _ _ _ _ _ _ _ _ _ _ _ _ _ _ _

   _____

   _____

   _ _ _ _ _ _ _ _ _ _ _ _ _ _ _ _ _

   _____

Communicating Results

Name: _____ Date: _____

Directions: Think of an animal you know. Draw the adult animal in one box and the baby animal in the other. Answer the question.

Adult Animal	**Baby Animal**

1. Talk to a friend about your two drawings.

Learning Content

Name: _____ **Date:** _____

Directions: Read the text. Answer the questions.

Lookalikes

Parents and kids can look alike. Twins can look exactly alike, though. This is because of traits. Traits are how a person looks and acts. They can come from your parents. Hair color is a trait. Some traits come from the environment. A tan is one of these traits.

1. What is a trait?

   a. hair color

   b. shirt color

   c. car color

   d. house color

2. Can twins have differences?

   a. yes

   b. no

Analyzing Data

Name: _____ **Date:** _____

Directions: Study the picture. Answer the questions.

curly hair

blue eyes

dimples

tanned skin

1. Which of these did the mom pass to the girl?

   a. tanned skin   **b.** blue eyes

   c. scar   **d.** bruise

2. Which of these is a trait that comes from the environment?

   a. tanned skin   **b.** blue eyes

   c. curly hair   **d.** dimples

Name: _____ **Date:** _____

Directions: Read the text. Answer the questions.

Jake and Jackson are identical twins. This means that they have the exact same traits from their parents. Jake loves to play outside. Jackson likes to play inside. Jake has freckles from the sun. Jackson does not.

Developing Questions

1. Why does Jake have freckles and Jackson does not?

   a. Jackson spends more time in the sun.

   b. Jake inherited freckles from his parents.

   c. Jackson does not want freckles.

   d. Jake spends more time in the sun.

2. What is a question you might ask about differences in identical twins?

   _____

   _____

   _____

   _____

Planning Solutions

Name: _____ **Date:** _____

Directions: Read the text. Answer the questions.

Jada and Kayla are sisters. They look a lot alike. They have straight hair and wear glasses. Jada has a scar on her hand.

1. What kind of trait is Jada's scar?

   a. an environmental trait

   b. a special trait

   c. an inherited trait

   d. a unique trait

2. How could you learn more about your traits?

_____

_ _

_____

_ _

_____

_ _

_____

Name: _____ Date: _____

Directions: Draw yourself and one of your family members. Label some traits you share. Label some that are different.

You	Family Member

Communicating Results

Learning Content

Name: _____ Date: _____

Directions: Read the text. Answer the questions.

How Does Sound Happen?

Sound is anything you can hear. Music is a sound. Car horns are sounds. Talking is a sound. Sound comes from vibrations. Vibrations are a quick motion back and forth. Vibrations make sound waves. Sound waves must move through matter, like air or water, to reach our ears.

1. What makes sounds?

   a. air   **b.** water

   c. vibrations   **d.** soil

2. What is an example of a sound?

   a. bumpy   **b.** sweet

   c. red   **d.** music

Name: _____ **Date:** _____

Directions: Study the picture. Answer the questions.

sound waves

Analyzing Data

1. In the picture, where is the sound coming from?

   a. the person   **b.** the ground

   c. the dog   **d.** the wind

2. What are the sound waves passing through?

   a. water   **b.** gel

   c. air   **d.** dirt

Developing Questions

Name: _____ **Date:** _____

Directions: Read the text. Answer the questions.

Maria loves music. She plays instruments at school. She plays a drum. She plays a tambourine. She plays a triangle, too. They all make different sounds. Some sound high. Some sound low.

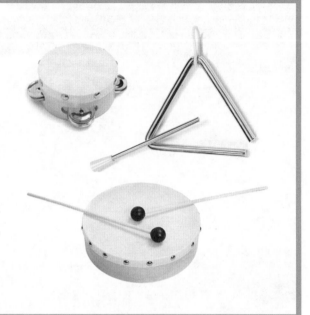

1. How can Maria tell that the instruments make different sounds?

   a. She hears them.   **b.** She sees them.

   c. She feels them.   **d.** She tastes them.

2. What is a question Maria could ask about the different sounds the instruments make?

   _____

   _____

   _____

   _____

Name: _____ **Date:** _____

Directions: Read the text. Answer the questions.

Maria plays instruments at school. They each have different sound waves. Some sound high. Some sound low. Maria wants to make her own.

1. Why do different instruments make different sounds?

   a. different sound waves

   b. the same sound waves

   c. different light waves

   d. different textures

2. How can Maria test the different sounds instruments can make?

   _____

   _____

   _____

   _____

   _____

   _____

Name: _____ **Date:** _____

Directions: Read the text. Circle the part of each object that vibrates.

Maria finds things at home that make sounds. She strums rubber bands. She beats the bottom of a pot. She taps two spoons together.

Communicating Results

Name: _____ **Date:** _____

Directions: Read the text. Answer the questions.

How Do Animals Make Sounds?

Animals make sounds with body parts. Sound comes from vibrations. Vibrations are quick motions back and forth. Dogs use their throats. Crickets rub their wings. Rattlesnakes shake their tails.

Learning Content

1. How do animals make sounds?

   a. instruments
   b. stereos
   c. talking
   d. body parts

2. What do crickets use to make sound?

   a. wings
   b. throats
   c. tails
   d. legs

Name: _____ Date: _____

Directions: Study the chart. Answer the questions.

Analyzing Data

Animal	**How It Makes Sound**
grasshopper	rubs legs together
rattlesnake	shakes tip of tail
elephant	trunk
dog	throat
frog	throat

1. What body part do elephants use to make sounds?

   a. throat   **b.** trunk

   c. legs   **d.** tail

2. Which animal uses its legs to make sound?

   a. rattlesnake   **b.** frog

   c. dog   **d.** grasshopper

51407—180 Days of Science

Name: _____ **Date:** _____

Directions: Read the text. Answer the questions.

Sahil is exploring near a pond. He sees a croaking frog. When the frog croaks, its throat expands like a balloon. Then its throat deflates. Its mouth does not open when it croaks.

Developing Questions

1. What expands when the frog makes sound?

   a. eyes   **b.** throat

   c. toes   **d.** stomach

2. What is a question Sahil could ask about how the frog makes sounds?

   _____

   -

   _____

   _____

   -

   _____

   _____

   -

   _____

Planning Solutions

Name: _____ **Date:** _____

Directions: Read the text. Answer the questions.

Jennifer has a cat. Its name is Snowflake. Snowflake purrs when she's happy. Her throat moves when she purrs. Jennifer wants to know what causes the purring sound.

1. What is another thing cats can do that makes sound?

   a. talk   **b.** whisper

   c. meow   **d.** shake their tail

2. Make a plan for Jennifer to feel the vibrations when she talks.

   _____

   _

   _____

   _

   _____

Name: _____ **Date:** _____

Directions: Look at the pictures. Write the sound that comes from each body part.

rattlesnake

_____

_____

cat

_____

_____

frog

_____

Learning Content

Name: _____ **Date:** _____

Directions: Read the text. Answer the questions.

Do You Hear How I Hear?

Our ears hear sounds. Sound waves are created by vibrations. When sound enters the ear, different parts of the ear move. The movements send signals to the brain. The brain knows what the signals mean.

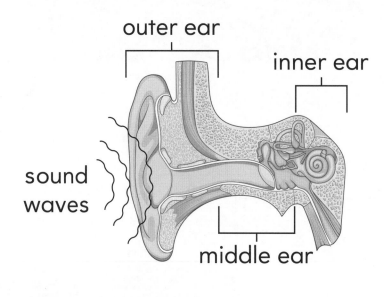

outer ear

inner ear

sound waves

middle ear

1. With which body part do we hear sound waves?

   a. eyes   **b.** ears

   c. nose   **d.** mouth

2. What does our brain turn into sound?

   a. inner ear   **b.** middle ear

   c. signals   **d.** ear lobe

Analyzing Data

Name: _____ **Date:** _____

Directions: Read the text. Study the picture. Answer the questions.

Sound enters our ear. Parts of the ear moves. Then signals are sent to the brain.

outer ear

inner ear

eardrum

signals to brain

sound

middle ear

1. In which part of the ear is the eardrum?

   a. outer   **b.** inner

   c. middle   **d.** sound

2. Where do sound waves enter the ear?

   a. inner ear   **b.** outer ear

   c. middle ear   **d.** eardrum

Name: _____ **Date:** _____

Directions: Read the text. Answer the questions.

Anisah is outside with her mom. It is cold. She is wearing earmuffs. Her mom says something. Anisah can't hear her very well. She takes off the earmuffs and can hear again.

1. Why does wearing earmuffs make things quieter for Anisah?

   a. It allows more sound waves to reach her ears.

   b. It blocks some of the sound waves.

   c. It blocks all the sound waves.

   d. It doesn't make things quieter.

2. What is a question Anisah can ask about the earmuffs?

   _____

   _____

   _____

   _____

51407—180 Days of Science

Planning Solutions

Name: _____ **Date:** _____

Directions: Read the text. Answer the questions.

> Luis loves music. Music is quiet when he is far away from his stereo. He wants to know why.

1. Why does the music sound different when Luis is far from his stereo?

   a. It is quieter.

   b. It is louder.

   c. It is faster.

   d. It is slower.

2. How can Luis test how loud his stereo is?

   _____

   _

   _____

   _

   _____

Name: _____ Date: _____

Directions: Look at the chart Luis made. Fill in the graph.

How I Listened	Volume
near music	5
far from music	1
wearing earmuffs	4
underwater	3

Listening and Sound Volume

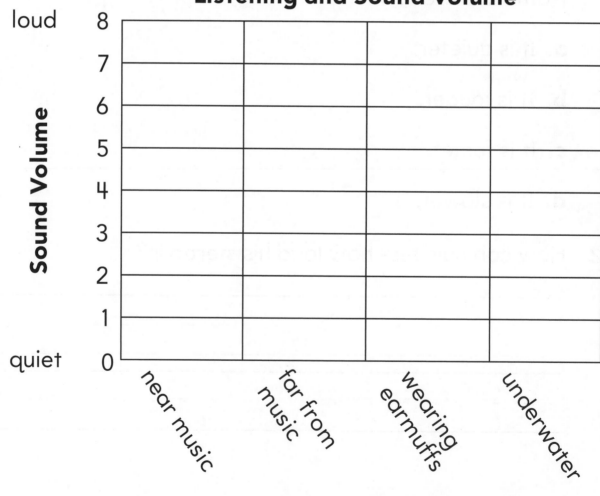

How I Listened

Name: _____ **Date:** _____

Directions: Read the text. Answer the questions.

Did You See That?

We use our eyes to see. Our eyes need light to see. When you are in a dark room, you can't see because there is no light. Light enters our eyes, and our eyes send signals to our brains. Our brains tell us what we are seeing.

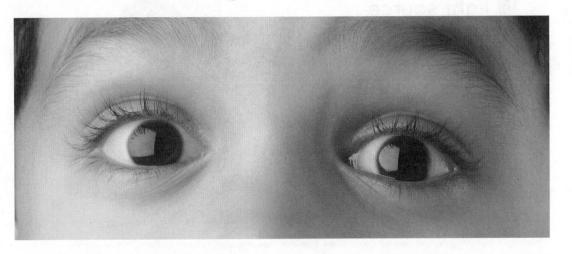

1. What do our eyes need to see?

   a. eyelids   **b.** darkness

   c. light   **d.** eyelashes

2. Which body part tells us what we are seeing?

   a. brain   **b.** ear

   c. nose   **d.** tongue

Analyzing Data

Name: _____ **Date:** _____

Directions: Read the text. Study the picture. Answer the questions.

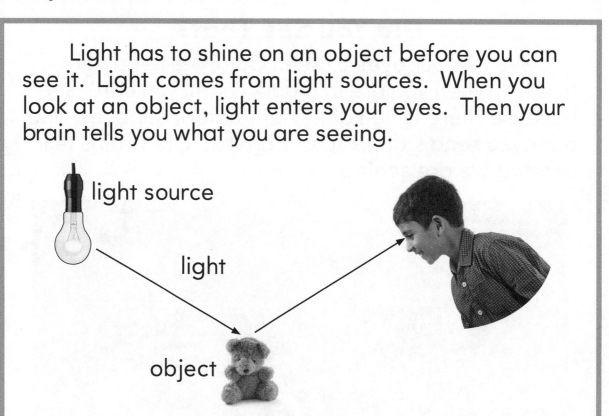

Light has to shine on an object before you can see it. Light comes from light sources. When you look at an object, light enters your eyes. Then your brain tells you what you are seeing.

light source

light

object

1. What is an example of a light source?

   a. a book   **b.** a lamp

   c. a wall   **d.** a mirror

2. Where does light come from?

   a. brain   **b.** teddy bears

   c. light sources   **d.** eyes

Name: _____ **Date:** _____

Directions: Read the text. Answer the questions.

Garett is playing in his room during a thunderstorm. The power goes out. The lights turn off. He can't see, so he turns on his flashlight. Now Garett can see where he aims his flashlight.

1. What is the flashlight?

   a. thunderstorm

   b. light source

   c. power

   d. toy

2. What is a question Garett could ask about light sources?

   _____

   _____

   _____

   _____

Name: _____ **Date:** _____

Directions: Read the text. Answer the questions.

Garett is playing in his room during a thunderstorm. The power goes out. The lights turn off. He sees flashes from the lightning. His room lights up when the lightning flashes.

1. What is the lightning?

   a. a light source

   b. a light bulb

   c. a flashlight

   d. sound waves

2. Should Garett use a flashlight or a night light to light his room? Why?

   _____

   _

   _____

   _

   _____

Name: _____ Date: _____

Directions: Circle the light source in each picture.

Communicating Results

Learning Content

Name: _____ **Date:** _____

Directions: Read the text. Answer the questions.

Who Turned on That Light?

Our eyes need light to see objects. Some things give off light. Some things reflect light. Things that give off light are called light sources. The sun, light bulbs, and candle flames are light sources. Teddy bears, bikes, and chairs all reflect light.

1. What reflects light?

   a. light bulb   **b.** chair

   c. sun   **d.** candle flame

2. What gives off light?

   a. teddy bear   **b.** bike

   c. sun   **d.** book

Name: _____ **Date:** _____

Directions: Read the text. Study the picture. Answer the questions.

Light sources give off light. The light goes straight into our eyes when we look at them. It is not reflecting off an object.

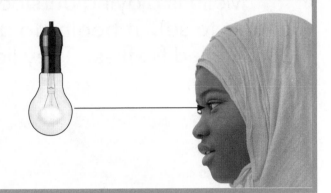

1. In the picture, what is giving off light?

   a. the eye

   b. the mouth

   c. the light bulb

   d. something not shown

2. How does light from a light source reach our eyes?

   a. Goes straight into our eyes.

   b. Reflects off a chair.

   c. Reflects off a book.

   d. Reflects off our eye.

Developing Questions

Name: _____ **Date:** _____

Directions: Read the text. Answer the questions.

> Malia is playing outside. It is summer. The sun begins to set. It begins to get dark. Malia sees bugs called fireflies. They light up. They look like tiny lights.
>
>

1. Why does it get dark when the sun sets?

   a. The sun is reflecting light.

   b. The sun is a light source.

   c. The fireflies are a light source.

   d. The fireflies are reflecting light.

2. What is a question Malia could ask about the fireflies?

   _____

   _____

   _____

   _____

Name: _____ **Date:** _____

Directions: Read the text. Answer the questions.

Malia is outside with her family. It gets dark. They see fireflies in the dark. They look like tiny lights. They don't give off enough light to light up the whole porch, though. Her dad turns on the porch light.

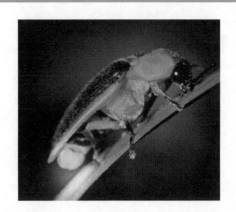

1. What else would create enough light for Malia's family to see outside?

   a. fireflies

   b. a camp fire

   c. a mirror

   d. a candle

2. How can Malia test to see which light sources are best for seeing outside at night?

   _____

   _____

   _____

   _____

Communicating Results

Name: ______________________ Date: __________

Directions: Read the text. Then draw pictures of four light sources. Answer the question.

1.	2.
3.	4.

1. What is a light source that you use every day?

____

____

Learning Content

Name: _____ **Date:** _____

Directions: Read the text. Answer the questions.

"Invisible" Ink

You can't see in the dark! Things are still there, though. There are other things that are invisible even when the lights are on. That means you can't see them. You can't see "invisible" ink unless you heat it. You can't see x-rays, but they take pictures of your bones. Even when you can't see something, there are ways to tell it's there.

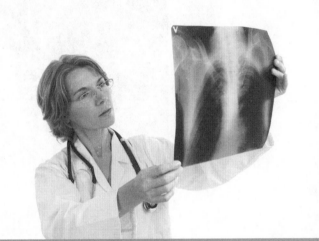

1. What does invisible mean?

   a. able to be seen   **b.** bright

   c. dark   **d.** unable to be seen

2. What can take pictures of your bones?

   a. x-rays   **b.** lights

   c. microwaves   **d.** sun rays

Analyzing Data

Name: _____ Date: _____

Directions: Read the text. Study the picture. Answer the questions.

> X-rays take pictures of your bones. Doctors use these pictures to see if your bones are healthy.

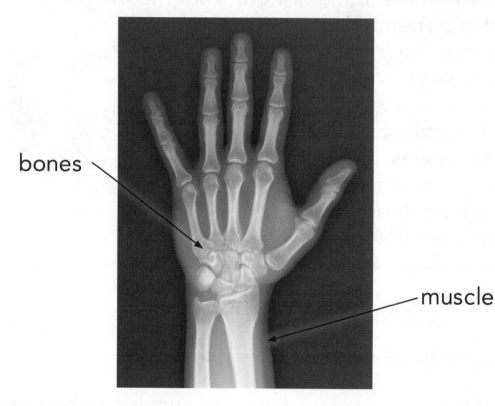

bones

muscle

1. What do x-rays show well?

   a. fingernails   **b.** bones

   c. skin color   **d.** hair color

2. What do x-rays show with less detail?

   a. muscle   **b.** freckles

   c. skin color   **d.** temperature

Name: _____ **Date:** _____

Directions: Read the text. Answer the questions.

> Mateo likes to read. The people in his books write with ink you can't see. They have to find ways to see the messages. Mateo wants to make some.

1. Can you ever see invisible ink?

　a. No, you can never see it.

　b. Yes, you can find ways to see it.

　c. Yes, you can always see it.

　d. It doesn't exist.

2. What is a question Mateo can ask about invisible ink?

_____

_____

_____

_____

Planning Solutions

Name: _____ **Date:** _____

Directions: Read the text. Answer the questions.

Mateo wants to make ink you can't see. You can use lemon juice and water to do this. To see the ink, you have to use heat. He has a flashlight, a glow stick, and a hair dryer.

1. What should Mateo use to heat up the invisible ink?

   a. the hair dryer

   b. the glow stick

   c. the flashlight

   d. something else

2. Would an envelope or a clear plastic bag work best to keep a note from being seen? Why?

   _____

   _____

   _____

   _____

Name: _____ **Date:** _____

Directions: Circle the objects you can use to make invisible ink. Answer the question.

ABC

1. When would you use invisible ink? Why?

_____

_____

_____

_____

Name: _____ **Date:** _____

Directions: Read the text. Answer the questions.

Hide and Seek

Some objects block light. When this happens, it makes a dark shadow. Things like wood, apples, and your body block light. Some things let light through. All light can go through clear glass. Tissue paper only lets some light through.

1. What makes a shadow?

   a. Some light going through.

   b. Blocked light.

   c. All light going through.

   d. Changing the color of light.

2. What would make a dark shadow?

   a. wood

   b. glass

   c. clear plastic

   d. water

Name: _____ **Date:** _____

Directions: Study the chart. Answer the questions.

Transparent		ALL light passes through
Translucent		SOME light passes through
Opaque		NO light passes through

1. Which object is translucent?

   a. an apple

   b. a tree

   c. glass

   d. tissue paper

2. What kind of object casts a dark shadow?

   a. opaque

   b. transparent

   c. translucent

   d. all of them

Name: _____ **Date:** _____

Directions: Read the text. Answer the questions.

Developing Questions

When Colby plays outside, she likes to watch her shadow. She notices that everything that blocks light creates a shadow.

1. Why does Colby's body make a shadow?

   a. It absorbs light.

   b. It blocks light.

   c. It lets light pass through.

   d. It doesn't make a shadow.

2. What can Colby ask about shadows?

   _____

   - - - - - - - - - - - - - - - - - -

   _____

   _____

   - - - - - - - - - - - - - - - - - -

   _____

   _____

   - - - - - - - - - - - - - - - - - -

   _____

Name: _____ **Date:** _____

Directions: Read the text. Answer the questions.

Colby is playing with a flashlight. She sees that light shines where she points it. She points the light at an apple. She points it at a clear plastic bottle. She points it at a window and tissue paper. It looks different each time.

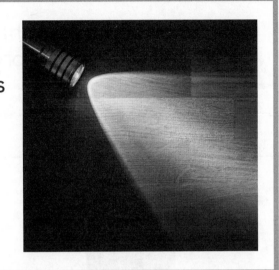

Planning Solutions

1. Which object would cast a dark shadow?

   a. the tissue paper

   b. the bottle

   c. the window

   d. the apple

2. How can Colby study transparent, translucent, and opaque objects?

   _____

   _ _ _ _ _ _ _ _ _ _ _ _ _ _ _ _

   _____

   _____

   _ _ _ _ _ _ _ _ _ _ _ _ _ _ _ _

   _____

Communicating Results

Name: _____ **Date:** _____

Directions: Read the text. Circle the correct answers.

Colby shined a light on different objects. She created a chart to record her findings.

Object	Type of Material
apple	transparent translucent opaque
window	transparent translucent opaque
tissue paper	transparent translucent opaque
clear plastic bottle	transparent translucent opaque

Name: _____ **Date:** _____

Directions: Read the text. Answer the questions.

Learning Content

Mirror Mirror

Light travels in a straight line until it hits an object. Some things let light pass through. Glass lets light through. Light can also be reflected. This means it bounces off of the object. Mirrors reflect all light. You can use a mirror to bounce a beam of light onto something else.

1. What is reflection?

   a. When light bounces off an object.

   b. When light is absorbed into an object.

   c. When light changes an object.

   d. When light passes through an object.

2. What reflects all light?

   a. an apple

   b. a mirror

   c. glass

   d. water

Analyzing Data

Name: _____ Date: _____

Directions: Read the text. Study the chart. Answer the questions.

> Some objects reflect light. Some let light through.

Object	What It Does
mirror	reflects all light
shiny metal	reflects most light
glass	lets light through

1. What does shiny metal do?

   a. Reflects most light.   **b.** Lets all light through.

   c. Lets some light through.   **d.** Reflects all light.

2. What does a mirror do?

   a. Reflects some light.   **b.** Absorbs light.

   c. Lets light pass through.   **d.** Reflects all light.

Name: _____ **Date:** _____

Directions: Read the text. Answer the questions.

> Light travels in a straight line. Sean can see this when he points a flashlight at a wall. When he points it at a mirror, it bounces off. He sees it shine on another wall.

Developing Questions

1. Why does the light shine where he points the flashlight?

   a. Light travels in a curve.

   b. Light travels in a straight line.

   c. Light travels in a zigzag.

   d. Light does not travel.

2. What can Sean ask about the flashlight and the mirror?

   _____

   _____

   _____

   _____

Planning Solutions

Name: _____ **Date:** _____

Directions: Read the text. Answer the questions.

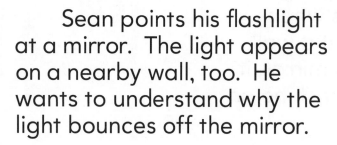 

Sean points his flashlight at a mirror. The light appears on a nearby wall, too. He wants to understand why the light bounces off the mirror.

1. How can Sean tell the light bounces off the mirror?

    a. It lights up the whole room.

    b. It shines only on the mirror.

    c. It shines on the mirror and wall.

    d. It shines on the wall and not the mirror.

2. How can Sean study light bouncing off objects?

    _____

    _____

    _____

    _____

Name: _____ **Date:** _____

Directions: Read the words in the box. Use them to label the diagram. Then, answer the question.

wall	light	flashlight

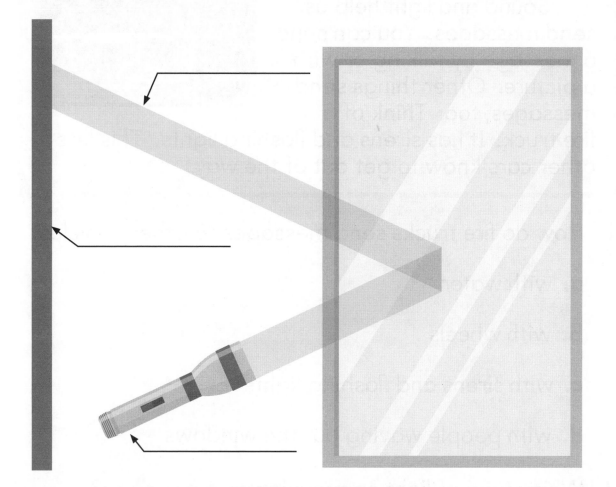

1. What happens when you point a flashlight at a mirror?

_____

_ _

_____

_____

_ _

_____

Communicating Results

Learning Content

Name: _____ **Date:** _____

Directions: Read the text. Answer the questions.

Seeing and Hearing a Message

Sound and light help us send messages. You can send a message by talking or with a picture. Other things send messages, too. Think of a fire truck. It has sirens and flashing lights. This lets other cars know to get out of the way.

1. How do fire trucks send messages to other vehicles?

    a. with water

    b. with wheels

    c. with sirens and flashing lights

    d. with people waving out the windows

2. Which type of light communicates a message?

    a. sunlight

    b. a lamp

    c. a street lamp

    d. a traffic light

Name: _____ **Date:** _____

Directions: Study the chart. Answer the questions.

Object	What It Does	Light or Sound?
traffic light	changes colors	light
ambulance	sirens, flashing lights	sound and light
drum	makes music	sound

1. What do the ambulance and the drum have in common?

   a. They use sound.   **b.** They are vehicles.

   c. They are the same color.   **d.** They use light.

2. Does a traffic light use light and sound?

   a. yes   **b.** no

Developing Questions

Name: _____ **Date:** _____

Directions: Read the text. Answer the questions.

Nika is on the cheerleading team. They cheer at basketball games. People in the front row cheer with them. People in the back row don't.

1. Why might the people in the back row not cheer?

   a. The cheers are too loud.

   b. They can't hear the cheerleaders.

   c. Their cheers are too exciting.

   d. The cheerleaders are close enough to see.

2. What is a question Nika can ask about the volume of her team's cheers?

   _____

   _ _ _ _ _ _ _ _ _ _ _ _ _ _ _ _ _ _

   _____

   _ _ _ _ _ _ _ _ _ _ _ _ _ _ _ _ _ _

   _____

Name: _____ **Date:** _____

Directions: Read the text. Answer the questions.

Nika is a cheerleader. She learned that people in the back can't hear their cheers well. She wants to know how more people can hear their cheers.

Planning Solutions

1. What should Nika focus on when trying to solve her team's problem?

   a. their pompoms

   b. their uniforms

   c. their cheer routine

   d. their volume

2. How can Nika's team help people in the back hear their cheers?

   _____

   _____

   _____

   _____

Communicating Results

Name: ______________________ Date: __________

Directions: Draw something that uses sound and light to send a message. Then, answer the question.

1. Why is it good to use *both* sound and light to send messages?

Name: _____ **Date:** _____

Directions: Read the text. Answer the questions.

Send a Signal

We can use light and sound to send messages. They can go long distances. They can go across town. They can go across the country. They can even go around the world. We can do this with technology. Computers, phones, and TVs all send messages. They use light and sound.

1. What can send a message to another state?

   a. sirens   **b.** walkie talkie

   c. drum   **d.** telephone

2. What uses light and sound?

   a. headphones   **b.** drum

   c. whispering   **d.** television

Analyzing Data

Name: _____ **Date:** _____

Directions: Read the text. Study the chart. Answer the questions.

Morse Code is used to send messages. Dots and dashes stand for letters. They can be made with sound or light. A telegraph can send messages far away with Morse Code. They sound like long and short clicks.

A	• ▬	N	▬ •
B	▬ • • •	O	▬ ▬ ▬
C	▬ • ▬ •	P	• ▬ ▬ •
D	▬ • •	Q	▬ ▬ • ▬
E	•	R	• ▬ •
F	• • ▬ •	S	• • •
G	▬ ▬ •	T	▬
H	• • • •	U	• • ▬
I	• •	V	• • • ▬
J	• ▬ ▬ ▬	W	• ▬ ▬
K	▬ • ▬	X	▬ • • ▬
L	• ▬ • •	Y	▬ • ▬ ▬
M	▬ ▬	Z	▬ ▬ • •

1. How is Morse Code used with a telegraph?

   a. sound

   b. light

   c. color

   d. taste

2. Which is the letter "C" in Morse Code?

   a. ▬ • ▬ •

   b. ▬ ▬

   c. ▬ ▬ • •

   d. • •

3. Write a three-letter word in Morse Code.

   _____

   _ _ _ _ _ _ _ _ _ _ _ _ _ _ _ _

   _____

Name: _____ **Date:** _____

Directions: Read the text. Answer the questions.

Mason's best friend lives next door. They play together every day. Now she is moving to another town. Mason wants to stay in touch with her.

1. How can Mason send his friend messages after she moves?

a. Wave out the window.

b. Use the phone.

c. Use a megaphone to talk.

d. Walk outside.

2. What can Mason ask about how he will talk to his friend?

_____

_ _ _ _ _ _ _ _ _ _ _ _ _ _ _ _ _ _ _ _

_____

_ _ _ _ _ _ _ _ _ _ _ _ _ _ _ _ _ _ _ _

_____

Planning Solutions

Name: _____ **Date:** _____

Directions: Read the text. Answer the questions.

> Mason's best friend moved away. He wants to see her every day. He wants to talk to her every day. He knows he needs something that uses light to see her. He knows he needs something that uses sound to hear her. Mason wants to know what he should use to do this.

1. Should Mason use light or sound to see and talk to his friend?

   a. light

   b. sound

   c. both

   d. neither

2. What is something Mason could use to solve his problem?

   _____

   _ _ _ _ _ _ _ _ _ _ _ _ _ _ _ _ _ _ _

   _____

   _ _ _ _ _ _ _ _ _ _ _ _ _ _ _ _ _ _ _

   _____

Name: _____ **Date:** _____

Directions: Some things send messages close by. Some send messages far away. Put an X in the correct boxes of the chart. Then, answer the question.

	Close By	**Far Away**
megaphone 		
headphones 		
walkie talkie 		

1. What is your favorite way to send messages? Why?

_____

_ _

_____

_ _

_____

Learning Content

Name: _____ Date: _____

Directions: Read the text. Answer the questions.

The Tin Can Telephone

Sound travels through air. It doesn't travel very far, though. Close people are easy to hear. They are quiet when they are far. A tin can telephone sends sound farther than air.

1. Why are far away people hard to hear?

   a. The sound doesn't travel very far.

   b. The sound travels too far.

   c. The sound travels too fast.

   d. The sound travels the wrong direction.

2. Why does a tin can telephone help you hear a person far away?

   a. It doesn't send sound very far.

   b. It stops sound.

   c. It sends sound farther.

   d. Sound bounces off it.

Name: _____ **Date:** _____

Directions: Read the text. Study the picture. Answer the questions.

> A tin can telephone is simple. Two cans are connected by a string. One person talks into a can. Another person listens. Sound moves across the string. You can hear it on the other side. The string helps sound travel farther.

sound travels

sound created

sound received

1. What does the sound move across in a tin can telephone?

   a. the people   **b.** the string

   c. the cans   **d.** the air

2. Can you hear someone farther away with the tin can telephone?

   a. yes   **b.** no

Developing Questions

Name: _____ **Date:** _____

Directions: Read the text. Answer the questions.

Leah is studying music. She learns that drums can be used to send messages because they can be very loud. Leah wants to try this.

1. Why can drums be used to send messages?

   a. They are quiet.

   b. They are shrill.

   c. They are rhythmic.

   d. They are loud.

2. What is a question Leah can ask about drums?

   _____

   _____

   _____

   _____

   _____

Name: _____ **Date:** _____

Directions: Read the text. Answer the questions.

Leah has a large, loud drum. She is playing with her friend in the backyard. Leah wants to use the drum to send messages to her friend.

1. How far away could Leah's friend hear the drum?

   a. in another state

   b. in another city

   c. on another street

   d. in another country

2. How can Leah create a message with drum beats?

   _____

   _____

   _____

   _____

   _____

Communicating Results

Name: _____ **Date:** _____

Directions: Draw yourself sending a message with a drum. Answer the question.

1. Should you use a loud or quiet drum sound to send a message?

_____

- - - - - - - - - - - - - - - - - - - -

_____

- - - - - - - - - - - - - - - - - - - -

_____

Name: _____ Date: _____

Directions: Read the text. Answer the questions.

In the Spotlight

People can use light to send messages. There are many ways to do this. Lighthouses help boats find their way. Spotlights shine on important things. You can use light for Morse Code. All of these can send messages to people far away.

1. You can use light to send messages in
_____ .

   a. spotlights   **b.** lighthouses

   c. Morse Code   **d.** people

2. People can use light to _____ .

   a. send messages   **b.** play music

   c. taste food   **d.** call someone

Analyzing Data

Name: _____ **Date:** _____

Directions: Study the chart. Answer the questions.

Type of Light	What It Does
lighthouse	Shows sailors dangerous areas in the dark.
spotlight	Shows us where to look for important things.
Morse Code	Sends a message with a pattern of flashing light.

1. Which should you use to say, "I need help."?

   a. spotlight **b.** Morse Code

   c. lighthouse **d.** none of these

2. Can a lighthouse send messages to many people at once?

   a. yes **b.** no

Name: _____ **Date:** _____

Directions: Read the text. Answer the questions.

Charlie is putting on a play.
One actor has a lot of lines. He
wants to make sure people look
at the actor.

1. What could Charlie use to make sure the audience
   looks at the actor while he is saying his lines?

   a. spotlight

   b. laser pointer

   c. lantern

   d. his finger

2. What is a question Charlie can ask about spotlights?

   _____

   _____

   _____

   _____

Planning Solutions

Name: _____ **Date:** _____

Directions: Read the text. Study the pictures. Answer the questions.

> Ava reads book about sailing. She sees a picture of a lighthouse on a rocky cliff. The cliff could hurt boats.

1. How does the lighthouse help sailors avoid danger?

   a. It shows them where it is.

   b. It plays a song.

   c. It plays a recorded message.

   d. It has a sign on it.

2. How can Ava use light to warn others about danger?

   _____

   _____

   _____

   _____

Name: _____ **Date:** _____

Directions: Draw a picture of yourself using light to send a message. Answer the question.

1. Explain your drawing.

_____

 — — — — — — — — — — — — — — — — — — —

_____

 — — — — — — — — — — — — — — — — — — —

_____

 — — — — — — — — — — — — — — — — — — —

_____

2. Talk to a friend about how you can use light to send a message.

Learning Content

Name: _____ Date: _____

Directions: Read the text. Answer the questions.

The Sun, Moon, and Stars

You can see the sun, moon, and stars in the sky. You can't see them all at the same time. They have different patterns you can see. You can watch the sun, moon, and stars to predict their patterns.

1. Where can you see the sun, moon, and stars?

   a. on the ground   **b.** under water

   c. in the sky   **d.** in a cave

2. How can you see patterns in the sun, moon, and stars?

   a. Watch them.   **b.** Listen to them.

   c. Touch them.   **d.** Close your eyes.

Name: _____ **Date:** _____

Directions: Read the text. Study the chart. Answer the questions.

> The sun, moon, and stars always exist. We can't see them at the same time. Stars can only be seen at night because it is too bright during the day.

Object	When it Can Be Seen
moon	sometimes night and sometimes day
stars	night
sun	day

1. Which is the only object that you can see at night and during the day?

   a. stars

   b. moon

   c. sun

   d. none

2. Why can't you see the stars during the day?

   a. It is too bright outside.

   b. It is too dark outside.

   c. The stars don't exist.

   d. The stars are too far away.

Name: _____ **Date:** _____

Directions: Read the text. Answer the questions.

> Tai and his dad like to watch the sunrise and sunset. Tai sees that the sun always sets in the west and rises in the east.
>
>

1. Will the sun set in the west next month?

    a. yes

    b. no

2. What is a question Tai could ask about the patterns he sees?

    _____

    _

    _____

    _____

    _

    _____

Planning Solutions

Name: _____ **Date:** _____

Directions: Read the text. Answer the questions.

Tai likes to watch the sun rise and set. He watches the location of the sun at different times during the day. It looks like it moves through the sky.

1. What does watching the path of the sun help Tai do?

   a. see patterns

   b. form predictions

   c. see patterns and form predictions

   d. nothing

2. How can Tai track the movement of the sun?

   _____

   _____

   _____

   _____

Communicating Results

Name: _____ **Date:** _____

Directions: Read Tai's notes about the movement of the sun. Label the diagram. Answer the question.

This morning, the sun rose in the east at 6:00 a.m. At noon, the sun was overhead. The sun set in the west at 8:00 p.m.

Sun's Path Across the Sky

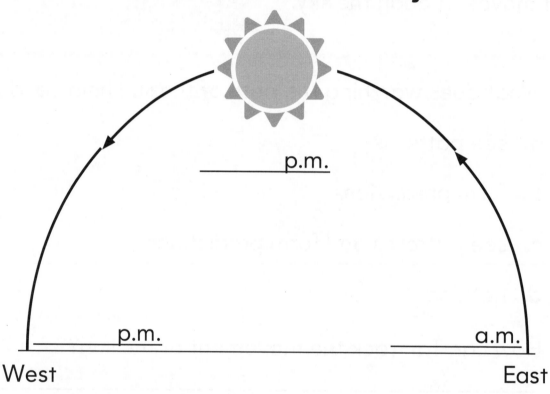

_____ p.m.

_____ p.m.   _____ a.m.

West   East

1. In which part of the sky do you predict the sun will rise the next day?

_____

_____

_____

_____

51407—180 Days of Science

Name: _____ **Date:** _____

Directions: Read the text. Answer the questions.

Patterns of the Sun and Moon

If you watch the sun and moon, you will notice patterns. Every day, the sun rises and sets. The moon seems to change shape during the month. You can predict what will happen by watching these patterns.

1. How often does the sun rise?

   a. every night   **b.** every day

   c. every week   **d.** every month

2. What will you notice if you watch the moon?

   a. It appears once a   **b.** It is always full.
   month.

   c. It seems to change   **d.** It never changes
   shape.   shape.

Name: _____ **Date:** _____

Directions: Read the text. Study the picture. Answer the questions.

The sun rises and sets every day. Shadows are long when the sun is low. Shadows are short when the sun is high.

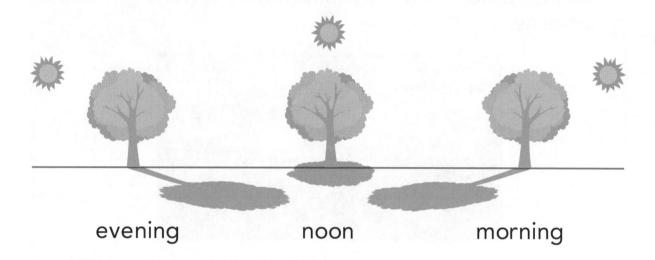

evening   noon   morning

1. When are shadows the longest?

   a. morning   **b.** afternoon

   c. noon   **d.** morning and evening

2. When are shadows the shortest?

   a. noon   **b.** morning

   c. evening   **d.** afternoon

Name: _____ **Date:** _____

Directions: Read the text. Answer the questions.

Amber looks at the moon one night. It is a small sliver. In a week, half the moon is showing. In another week, the moon is full.

Developing Questions

1. What can Amber tell from watching the moon?

    a. It appears to change shape.

    b. It always looks the same.

    c. It looks like a square.

    d. It changes colors.

2. What can Amber ask about the moon's changes?

    _____

    _____

    _____

    _____

    _____

Planning Solutions

Name: _____ **Date:** _____

Directions: Read the text. Answer the questions.

Amber looks at the moon over a month. First, the moon is a thin sliver. Eventually, it is a full circle. At the end of the month, it is a thin sliver again.

1. What is Amber seeing?

   a. a pattern

   b. different colors

   c. a square moon

   d. a star

2. Write a plan for tracking the moon's changes.

   _____

   _____

   _____

   _____

Name: _____ **Date:** _____

Directions: Read the text. Fill in the chart. Answer the question.

The sun doesn't always rise or set at the same time. Look at the other days to figure out the times.

Date	Sunrise	Sunset
January 17	7:31 a.m.	5:45 p.m.
January 18		5:46 p.m.
January 19	7:29 a.m.	

1. What time do you think the sun will rise on January 21? Why?

_____

_____

_____

_____

_____

_____

Communicating Results

Learning Content

Name: _____ **Date:** _____

Directions: Read the text. Answer the questions.

The Earth and Sun

The sun is a star. It is the closest star to Earth. The sun gives off light and warms Earth. People, plants, and animals can't live without the sun. The sun rises in the east every day. It sets in the west.

1. What is the sun?

    a. a planet   **b.** a star

    c. a lightbulb   **d.** a comet

2. Does the sun have a pattern?

    a. Yes, it rises in the east and sets in the west.   **b.** No, you never know where it will rise.

Name: _____ **Date:** _____

Directions: Study the chart. Answer the questions.

Time of Day	Where Is the Sun?
morning	in the east
noon	overhead
afternoon	in the west
night	not visible

1. When is the sun not visible?

   a. morning **b.** afternoon

   c. night **d.** noon

2. When is the sun in the east?

   a. morning **b.** noon

   c. afternoon **d.** another time

Developing Questions

Name: _____ Date: _____

Directions: Read the text. Study the picture. Answer the questions.

> Mike's class looks at the sun's location in the morning. They look again at noon. Then they look in the afternoon. The sun is in a different spot each time.

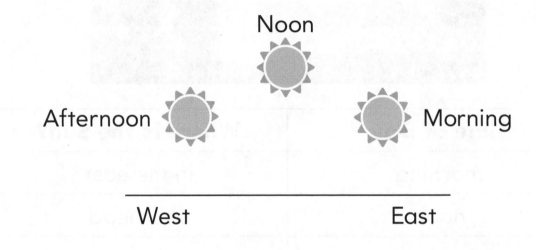

Noon

Afternoon

Morning

West   East

1. What pattern does Mike see with the sun?

    a. movement east to west   **b.** jumping

    c. changing color   **d.** blinking

2. What can Mike ask about the movement of the sun?

_____

_____

_____

_____

Planning Solutions

Name: _____ **Date:** _____

Directions: Read the text. Answer the questions.

Mike looks at the sky three times in one day. He sees that the sun looks like it is moving across the sky. Mike wants to see if the sun's movement has a pattern.

1. How can Mike find out if there is a pattern?

   a. Watch the sun's location the next day.

   b. Watch the moon's location the next day.

   c. Watch the stars' location the next day.

   d. Watch the clouds' location the next day.

2. Write a plan for tracking the sun's patterns.

   _____

   _____

   _____

   _____

3. Talk to a friend about your plan.

Name: _____ Date: _____

Communicating Results

Directions: Look at the chart Mike created. Draw the sun in the right spots. Answer the question.

Time	Sun's Location
6:00 a.m.	over the tree
12:00 p.m.	over the house
4:00 p.m.	over the bushes

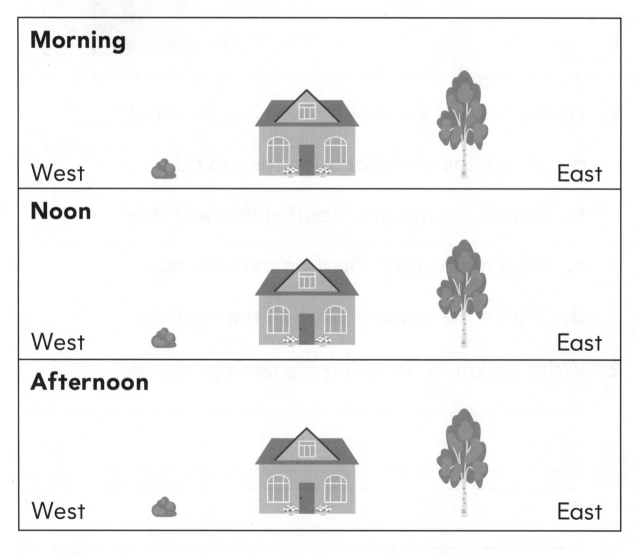

Morning

West   East

Noon

West   East

Afternoon

West   East

1. Tell a friend why you think the sun moves across the sky.

Name: _____ Date: _____

Directions: Read the text. Answer the questions.

The Seasons and the Sun

Seasons change. Sometimes the sun sets early. Sometimes it sets late. It can be hot or cold. You can see these changes all year.

1. Does the sun always set early?

   a. yes

   b. no

2. When can you see seasons change?

   a. All year long.

   b. Only at night.

   c. Only on Wednesdays.

   d. Only in summer.

3. Talk to a friend about why you think the seasons change.

Name: _____ **Date:** _____

Directions: Study the chart. The chart shows temperatures in a town. Answer the questions.

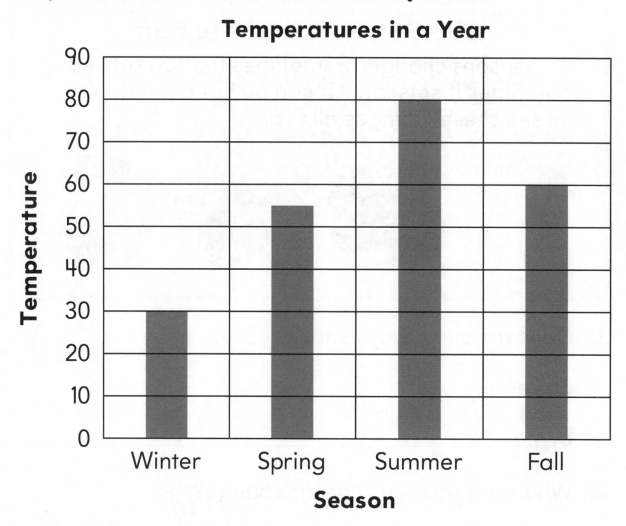

Temperatures in a Year

1. When is it the hottest?

   a. spring   **b.** winter

   c. summer   **d.** fall

2. Do spring and fall have similar temperatures?

   a. yes   **b.** no

Name: _____ **Date:** _____

Directions: Read the text. Answer the questions.

> It is winter, so the sun sets early. There are fewer hours of daylight in winter. Alex wants to play outside after dinner. It is six o'clock. Her mom says it is too dark. In the summer, she plays outside later.

1. Why is it dark after dinner?

   a. The sun sets early.   **b.** The sun sets late.

   c. The sun wasn't out.   **d.** The sun never sets.

2. What can Alex ask about the amount of daylight?

   _____

   _

   _____

   _

   _____

Planning Solutions

Name: _____ **Date:** _____

Directions: Read the text. Answer the questions.

Alex likes to play outside all year. In winter, the days seem short. There is less daylight. In summer, the days seem long. There is more daylight. Alex wants to know why this happens.

1. How is summer different?

    a. The days are longer.   **b.** The days are shorter.

    c. The days are the same.   **d.** The days are colder.

2. How can Alex track the amount of daylight in each season?

_____

_____

_____

_____

3. Talk to a friend about how daylight changes.

Name: _____ **Date:** _____

Directions: Read the text. Fill in the chart. Answer the question.

> Summer days have more hours of daylight. Winter days have fewer.

Hours of Daylight	Summer or Winter
9	
14	
8	
13	

1. Which season has shorter days?

_____

_ _

_ _

Communicating Results

Learning Content

Name: _____ **Date:** _____

Directions: Read the text. Answer the questions.

Which Way Does the Sun Go?

The sun rises and sets every day. It rises in the east. It sets in the west. The time the sun rises and sets changes. Sometimes the sun is lower in the sky. Sometimes it is high.

1. Where does the sun rise?

   a. In the east.   **b.** In the west.

   c. In the north.   **d.** In the south.

2. Where does the sun set?

   a. In the north.   **b.** In the south.

   c. In the east.   **d.** In the west.

3. Talk to a friend about why you think the sun rises in the east.

Name: _____ **Date:** _____

Directions: Read the text. Study the picture. Answer the questions.

Analyzing Data

> The sun always moves from east to west. The sun's path is highest in the sky during summer. It is lowest in the sky during winter.

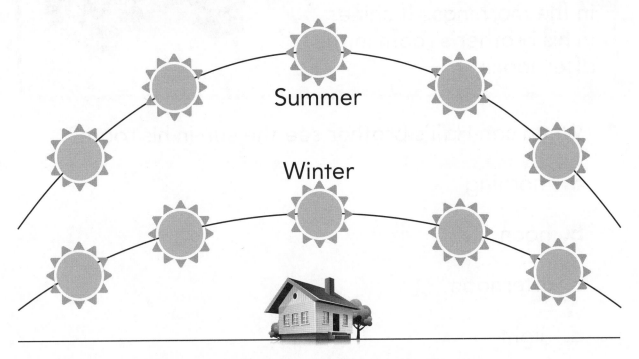

1. When is the sun lowest in the sky?

   a. spring

   b. winter

   c. summer

   d. fall

2. When is the sun highest in the sky?

   a. fall

   b. spring

   c. summer

   d. winter

Name: _____ Date: _____

Directions: Read the text. Answer the questions.

> The sun rises in the east. It shines in Haji's window in the mornings. It wakes him up. The sun doesn't shine in his brother's room in the mornings. It shines in his brother's room in the afternoons.

1. When can Haji's brother see the sun in his room?

   a. morning

   b. noon

   c. afternoon

   d. night

2. What could Haji ask about the sun's path?

   _____

   _____

   _____

   _____

3. Tell a friend what you know about the sun's path.

Name: _____ **Date:** _____

Directions: Read the text. Answer the questions.

Haji goes outside in the morning. He looks at a tree's shadow. The shadow is on the left of the tree. He goes out in the afternoon. The shadow is on the right of the tree.

Planning Solutions

1. Why did the shadow change places?

    a. The sun moved.   **b.** The tree moved.

    c. It didn't change.   **d.** It was in two places at once.

2. How can he use shadows to learn about the sun?

    _____

    _

    _____

    _

    _____

Earth and Space Science

Name: _____ Date: _____

Directions: Read the text. Match the time of day with the shadow. Answer the question.

> The sun rises in the east. It sets in the west. Shadows change position with the sun.

Morning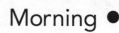

West _____ East

Noon •

West _____ East

Afternoon •

West _____ East

1. Can the sun help you tell time? Why or why not?

_____

_____

_____

_____

Name: _____ Date: _____

Directions: Read the text. Answer the questions.

The Earth and the Moon

The moon is the brightest object in the sky after the sun. It is also the closest object to Earth. The moon can often be seen at night. Sometimes it can be seen during the day. The same side of the moon always faces Earth.

1. What is the brightest object in the sky?

   a. the sun

   b. the moon

   c. the stars

   d. comets

2. What is the closest object to Earth?

   a. the moon

   b. the sun

   c. stars

   d. Jupiter

Analyzing Data

Name: _____ **Date:** _____

Directions: The moon rises and sets at different times. Study the chart. Answer the questions.

Moon Phase	Moonrise	Moonset
new	7:00 a.m.	7:00 p.m.
first quarter	noon	midnight
full	7:00 p.m.	7:00 a.m.

1. Which phase of the moon rises at noon?

   a. last quarter   **b.** new

   c. full   **d.** first quarter

2. Which phase of the moon isn't out at night?

   a. new   **b.** last quarter

   c. full   **d.** first quarter

Name: _____ **Date:** _____

Directions: Read the text. Answer the questions.

Cruz looks at the moon. Two hours later, it is farther west. Two hours after that, it's even farther west.

Developing Questions

1. Where do you predict the moon will be two hours after Cruz last looked at it?

   a. farther west   **b.** the same place

   c. farther east   **d.** where it started

2. What could Cruz ask about the moon's path?

   _____

   _____

   _____

   _____

3. Tell a friend something about the moon you have seen.

Planning Solutions

Name: _____ **Date:** _____

Directions: Read the text. Answer the questions.

Cruz watches when the moon rise for three nights. It rises at a different time each night. He wants to guess when it will rise the next night.

1. Do you predict that the moon will rise at a different time the next night?

   a. yes   **b.** no

2. How can he predict when the moon will rise the next day?

   _____

   _____

   _____

   _____

Name: _____ Date: _____

Directions: Think of the last time you saw the moon. Draw a picture of it. Then, answer the question.

[empty drawing box]

1. Tell a friend about patterns you have seen with the moon.

Learning Content

Name: _____ **Date:** _____

Directions: Read the text. Answer the questions.

Phases of the Moon

The moon revolves around Earth. It takes about 27 days to go around Earth. The moon reflects light from the sun. It looks like it changes shape. It doesn't actually change shape, though. The different shapes are called phases.

1. What are the shapes of the moon called?

   a. moon phases   **b.** shapes

   c. suns   **d.** rotations

2. How long is the moon's trip around Earth?

   a. 30 days   **b.** 25 days

   c. 14 days   **d.** 27 days

Name: _____ **Date:** _____

Directions: Read the text. Study the pictures. Answer the questions.

Each moon phase looks different. You can either see the whole moon, part of it, or none of it.

Moon Phases

new moon

waxing crescent

first quarter

waxing gibbous

full moon

waning gibbous

last quarter

waning crescent

1. Which phase of the moon shows just a sliver?

   a. waxing crescent   **b.** waning gibbous

   c. full   **d.** new

2. Which phase of the moon shows a full circle?

   a. full   **b.** new

   c. last quarter   **d.** first quarter

Developing Questions

Name: _____ Date: _____

Directions: Read the text. Answer the questions.

> Neela goes outside to look at the full moon. The next week, she looks again. She sees the moon is a different shape. She thinks the moon is in a different phase.

1. How does she know the moon is in a new phase?

    a. It's red.

    b. It's the same.

    c. It's gone.

    d. It's a different shape.

2. What could Neela ask about the moon's phases?

    _____

    _

    _____

    _

    _____

Name: _____ **Date:** _____

Directions: Read the text. Answer the questions.

> David wants to see a full moon. He knows that it takes about 27 days for the moon to complete a cycle.
>
>

1. What does David need to know to see the next full moon?

   a. when the last full moon happened

   b. what time the moon rises

   c. what time the moon sets

   d. what time the sun rises

2. How can David track the moon's phases?

_____

_____

_____

_____

ABC

Communicating Results

Name: _____ **Date:** _____

Directions: Look at the moon phases. Answer the questions.

Moon Phases

new
moon

waxing
crescent

first
quarter

waxing
gibbous

full
moon

waning
gibbous

last
quarter

waning
crescent

1. How is a new moon different from a full moon?

_____

- -

_____

- -

_____

2. How does the moon appear to change during the month?

_____

- -

_____

_____

- -

_____

3. Talk to your friend about a time you saw a full moon.

Name: _____ **Date:** _____

Directions: Read the text. Answer the questions.

Life on the Moon?

The moon is very different from Earth. The surface is covered in craters. People can't live on the moon. There are no plants or animals.

You can see the moon with the naked eye. A telescope will give you a better look, though.

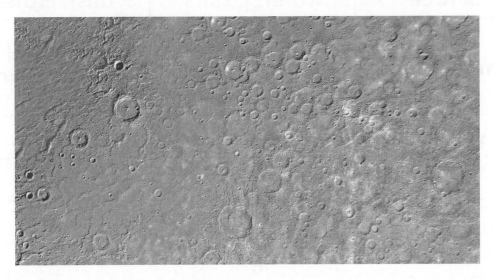

1. What lives on the moon?

   a. people

   b. plants

   c. animals

   d. nothing

2. What can give you a good look at the moon?

   a. a telescope

   b. reading glasses

   c. a magnifying glass

   d. a microscope

Name: _____ **Date:** _____

Directions: Read the text. Study the chart. Answer the questions.

> The moon does not have the things needed to support life. Earth does have what is needed.

	Earth	**Moon**
Surface	water, plants	dust, craters
Temperature	the right temperature for life	too hot and too cold for life
Water	yes	no
Air	yes	no

1. Why can't you breathe on the moon?

   a. There is no water.

   b. There is no air.

   c. There are no animals.

   d. There is dust.

2. Can plants grow on the moon?

   a. yes

   b. no

Name: _____ **Date:** _____

Directions: Read the text. Answer the questions.

Matt has a telescope. He uses it to look at the moon. He sees a gray surface and lots of dark spots. His mom shows him a picture of Earth from space. It is blue with swirls of white. His mom says the blue is water and the white swirls are clouds.

1. Does the moon look the same as Earth?

   a. yes   **b.** no

2. What could Matt ask about the moon?

   _____

   _____

   _____

   _____

Name: _____ **Date:** _____

Directions: Read the text. Answer the questions.

> Matt uses a telescope to look at the moon. He does not see blue water or green plants. The moon is gray and cratered. He thinks that the moon is different from Earth.

1. What is missing from the moon?

   a. water

   b. dust

   c. craters

   d. gray surface

2. How can Matt learn more about the moon?

   _____

   _____

   _____

   _____

Name: _____ **Date:** _____

Directions: Label craters on the moon. Label water and land on Earth. Answer the questions.

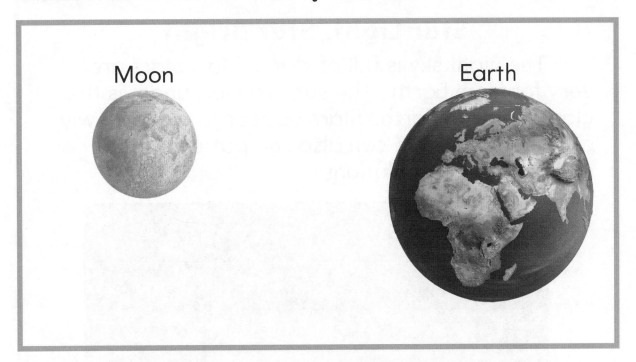

Moon   Earth

1. What is different about the moon and Earth?

   _____

   _____

   _____

   _____

2. Why can't you live on the moon?

   _____

   _____

   _____

   _____

Learning Content

Name: _____ Date: _____

Directions: Read the text. Answer the questions.

Star Light, Star Bright

The night sky is full of stars. Most stars are very far from Earth. The sun is a star, and it is the closest star to Earth. Stars appear to move slowly across the sky. We can also see patterns in the stars called constellations.

1. Most stars are _____ Earth.

   a. very far from   **b.** very close to

   c. somewhat close to   **d.** attached to

2. What are patterns of stars called?

   a. constellations   **b.** the sun

   c. Earth   **d.** sky

Name: _____ **Date:** _____

Directions: Read the text. Study the chart. Answer the questions.

Analyzing Data

> The North Star is one of the easiest stars to find. It is always in the north. You can use constellations to find it. It's near the Big Dipper. It's part of the Little Dipper.

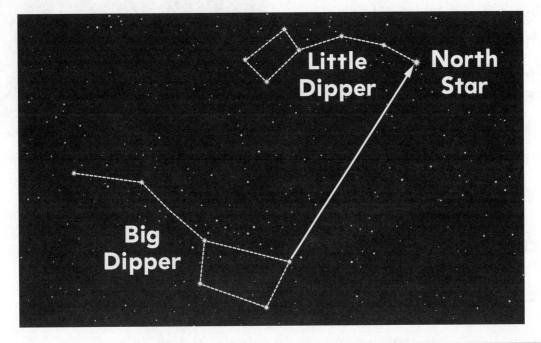

1. Where is the North Star?

   a. In the Big Dipper.   **b.** In the south.

   c. In the Little Dipper.   **d.** In the west.

2. What is the Big Dipper?

   a. constellation   **b.** North Star

   c. Little Dipper   **d.** the sun

Name: _____ **Date:** _____

Developing Questions

Directions: Read the text. Answer the questions.

Elle looks at the stars with her dad. She sees a pattern of stars. It's the constellation Leo. Two hours later, she finds it again. It appeared to move to a new spot.

1. What are patterns in the stars called?

   a. night

   b. sun

   c. constellations

   d. sky

2. What could Elle ask about the stars moving?

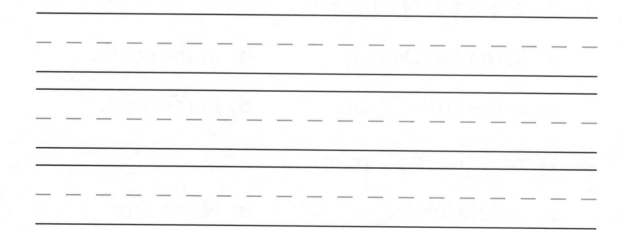

Name: _____ **Date:** _____

Directions: Read the text. Answer the questions.

Elle watches the stars at night. She compares the stars she sees. Some are much brighter. Some look bigger. Some are in groups. She wants to learn more about stars.

1. What can Elle see from looking at the stars?

   a. They're all different.   **b.** They're all the same.

   c. They're equally spaced.   **d.** They are all dim.

2. How can Elle track the stars with her journal?

   _____

   _____

   _____

   _____

Planning Solutions

Name: _____ **Date:** _____

Directions: Read the text. Draw a picture of the night sky. Answer the question.

Stars don't all look the same. Some are bright, and some are dim. Some are bigger, and some are smaller.

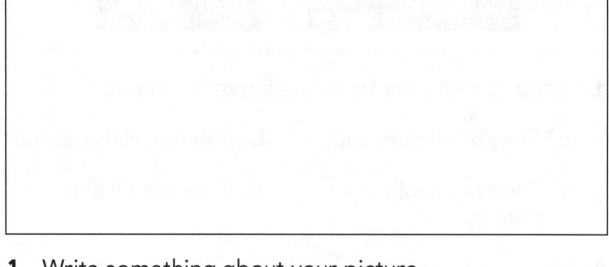

1. Write something about your picture.

_____

_ _

_____

_ _

_____

Name: _____ **Date:** _____

Directions: Read the text. Answer the questions.

Wonder What They Are?

Stars are the points of light you see in the night sky. They are not all the same, though. Some are bigger. Some are smaller. Some are brighter. Some are dimmer. Some are hotter. Some are cooler. They can be different colors, too.

1. Where can you see stars?

   a. sky during the day   **b.** underwater

   c. night sky   **d.** inside your house

2. How do stars differ?

   a. size   **b.** color

   c. temperature   **d.** all of these

Analyzing Data

Name: _____ **Date:** _____

Directions: Read the text. Study the pictures. Answer the questions.

> We can only see the stars at night. It is too bright during the day.

Night

Day

1. When can you see the stars?

    a. night   **b.** day

    c. day and night   **d.** never

2. What affects when you can see the stars?

    a. how hot it is   **b.** how cold it is

    c. how bright it is   **d.** what season it is

Name: _____ **Date:** _____

Directions: Read the text. Answer the questions.

> Jack is pretending that the lights in his room are the sun. He pretends that a flashlight is a star. When the lights are on, he can't see the "star."

1. Why can't he see the "star" when his lights are on?

   a. It's too bright.

   b. It's too dark.

   c. He can see it.

   d. The flashlight is too big.

2. What could Jack ask about the stars?

   _____

   _____

   _____

   _____

Name: _____ **Date:** _____

Directions: Read the text. Answer the questions.

Jack likes to look at the stars with his dad. They live in the city. It is hard to see the stars because there is a lot of light. When they go to the country, the stars are brighter.

1. Why are the stars harder to see in the city?

   a. It's colder.   **b.** It's brighter.

   c. It's darker.   **d.** It's warmer.

2. How can Jack create a model to show how light affects how bright stars look?

   _____

   _____

   _____

   _____

Planning Solutions

Name: _____ **Date:** _____

Directions: The way the stars look depend on how bright it is. Look at the chart. Answer the question.

Situation	Stars
daytime	not visible
night with lots of lights from buildings	dim
night with few lights from buildings	bright

1. How do the stars look from your home?

_____

_____

_____

2. How would the stars look at night in a place far from cities and towns?

_____

_____

_____

Communicating Results

Name: _____ **Date:** _____

Directions: Read the text. Answer the questions.

Counting the Stars

When you look at the sky at night, what do you see? Many, many stars. Can you count them? Probably not. There are so many stars in the universe, they can't be counted. They are also grouped together. They are not spaced evenly.

1. How many stars are there?

   a. 100

   b. 75

   c. 200

   d. Too many to count.

2. Are the stars evenly spaced?

   a. Yes, they are spaced evenly.

   b. No, they are spaced unevenly.

Name: _____ **Date:** _____

Directions: Read the text. Study the pictures. Answer the questions.

> Many stars are grouped together in the sky. Some are called constellations. They make patterns. They can look like animals or people. They can look like pretend creatures. They each have their own name.

Analyzing Data

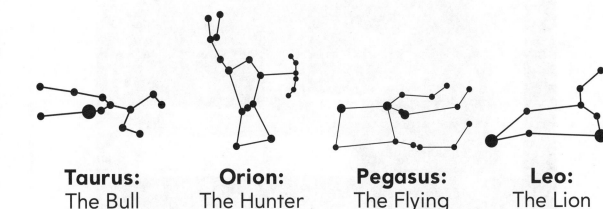

Taurus:
The Bull

Orion:
The Hunter

Pegasus:
The Flying
Horse

Leo:
The Lion

1. Which constellation shows a pretend creature?

   a. Pegasus   **b.** Taurus

   c. Orion   **d.** Leo

2. Which constellation shows a person?

   a. Leo   **b.** Pegasus

   c. Orion   **d.** Taurus

Name: _____ **Date:** _____

Directions: Read the text. Answer the questions.

Developing Questions

> Fletcher likes to look at the stars. The stars look grouped together. They are not spaced evenly. He tries to count them, but there are too many.

1. Can Fletcher count all the stars?

   a. Yes, if he tries.　　　**b.** No, there are too many.

2. What could Fletcher ask about the stars?

   _____

   _

   _____

   _

   _____

Name: _____ **Date:** _____

Directions: Read the text. Answer the questions.

Fran likes to read about space. She likes looking at stars. She is learning about constellations. She wants to find Taurus in the sky.

1. What does she need to know about Taurus to find it?

   a. What it looks like.   **b.** What color it is.

   c. What it sounds like.   **d.** Why it was named Taurus.

2. Make a plan for Fran to learn about constellations.

   _____

   _____

   _____

   _____

Planning Solutions

Name: _____ **Date:** _____

Directions: Read the text. Draw at least three stars and name them. Answer the question.

ABC

Communicating Results

> Stars can be named for where they are. They can also be named after the person who found them.

---

1. Why did you choose the names you did?

_____

_____

_____

_____

Name: _____ Date: _____

Directions: Read the text. Answer the questions.

Starbursts!

When you look at the stars, they don't all look the same. Some seem bright. Others are barely visible. Many of them look like they twinkle. This means that they switch between bright and faint.

1. Are stars all the same brightness?

    a. yes   **b.** no

2. If a star switches between bright and faint, it is _____ .

    a. dancing   **b.** jumping

    c. wiggling   **d.** twinkling

Name: _____ **Date:** _____

Directions: Study the chart. Answer the questions.

Analyzing Data

Situation	Can You See the Stars?
night, clear sky	yes
day	no
night, cloudy sky	no

1. Can we see the stars at night if it is cloudy?

   a. yes   **b.** no

2. Why can't we see the stars during the day?

   a. It's too bright.   **b.** It's too dark.

   c. It's too hot.   **d.** It's too cold.

3. Tell a friend about stars you've seen.

51407—180 Days of Science   © *Shell Education*

Name: _____ **Date:** _____

Directions: Read the text. Answer the questions.

When Mato looks at the stars, they are different. Some are bright. Some are dim. He thinks the bright ones are closer. The stars also look like they twinkle.

1. Do all the stars look the same?

   a. Yes, they are all very bright.

   b. No, some are bright, and some are dim.

2. What could Mato ask about the twinkling stars?

   _____

   _____

   _____

   _____

Planning Solutions

Name: _____ **Date:** _____

Directions: Read the text. Answer the questions.

> Mato watches the stars with his brother at night. They look like they twinkle. The moon doesn't twinkle, though. Mato's brother wants to know why the stars twinkle and the moon doesn't.

1. What looks like it twinkles in the sky?

   a. birds   **b.** clouds

   c. the moon   **d.** stars

2. How can they make a model of a twinkling star?

   _____

   _____

   _____

   _____

Name: _____ Date: _____

Directions: Read the text. Look at the pictures. Answer the questions.

> We can't see the stars during the day.
> Sometimes we can't see them at night either.

Communicating Results

1. Why might the stars not be visible at night?

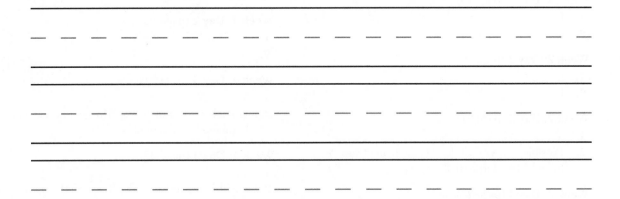

_____

_ _

_____

_ _

_____

_ _

_____

2. Do the stars still exist if we can't see them?

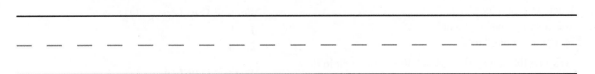

_____

_ _

_____

Answer Key

Life Science

Week 1: Day 1 (page 14)
1. b
2. a

Week 1: Day 2 (page 15)
1. a
2. b
3. a

Week 1: Day 3 (page 16)
1. a
2. Possible answer includes, "How much water does it need?"

Week 1: Day 4 (page 17)
1. a
2. Possible answer includes, "The same time because then she will see which food her cat chooses."

Week 1: Day 5 (page 18)
1. Rice: Circle not filled in
   Chicken: Half of circle filled in
   Fish: Circle filled in
2. Fish because the cat ate it all.

Week 2: Day 1 (page 19)
1. b
2. a

Week 2: Day 2 (page 20)
1. a
2. b

Week 2: Day 3 (page 21)
1. a
2. Possible answer includes, "Is the helmet supposed to look like a turtle shell?"

Week 2: Day 4 (page 22)
1. a
2. Possible answer includes, "Because the thorns can hurt you."

Week 2: Day 5 (page 23)
Duck: Webbed feet
Sparrow: Not webbed feet
Penguin: Webbed feet
1. Possible answer includes, "Because they help the birds swim."

Week 3: Day 1 (page 24)
1. b
2. b

Week 3: Day 2 (page 25)
1. a
2. b

Week 3: Day 3 (page 26)
1. a
2. Possible answer includes, "The plants on one side have brown leaves. The plants on the other side have green leaves."

Week 3: Day 4 (page 27)
1. a
2. Possible answer includes, "Find out how much water each plant gets. Give them both the same amount and see if the brown plants turn green."

Week 3: Day 5 (page 28)
Plants on the Left: brown, bright sun all day, little water
Plants on the Right: green, bright sun all day, lots of water
1. Possible answer includes, "More water because the green plants get more water."

Week 4: Day 1 (page 29)
1. a
2. b

Week 4: Day 2 (page 30)
1. b
2. b

Week 4: Day 3 (page 31)
1. a
2. Possible answer includes, "How could Angela tell her mom baked a treat?"

Week 4: Day 4 (page 32)
1. a
2. Possible answers include, "Blow on them," or "Put an ice cube in it."

Week 4: Day 5 (page 33)
Drawings will vary but should have two eyes, two ears, one nose, two hands, one mouth, and two legs.

Week 5: Day 1 (page 34)
1. b
2. a

Week 5: Day 2 (page 35)
1. b
2. a

Answer Key *(cont.)*

Week 5: Day 3 (page 36)
1. b
2. Possible answer includes, "How long will the sprout take to grow into a mature plant?"

Week 5: Day 4 (page 37)
1. b
2. Possible answer includes, "Look at a plant that is already grown up."

Week 5: Day 5 (page 38)
1—seed
2—seed with root
3—sprout
4—seedling
5—grown up plant
6—flower

Week 6: Day 1 (page 39)
1. b
2. d

Week 6: Day 2 (page 40)
1. c
2. c

Week 6: Day 3 (page 41)
1. b
2. Possible answer includes, "Why did the bug choose that leaf to lay eggs?"

Week 6: Day 4 (page 42)
1. b
2. Possible answer includes, "Photos because they show what the bug actually looks like in different stages."

Week 6: Day 5 (page 43)

| egg | larva | pupa | adult |

1. Possible answers include, "Lay eggs," or "Find food."

Week 7: Day 1 (page 44)
1. a
2. c

Week 7: Day 2 (page 45)
1. b
2. a

Week 7: Day 3 (page 46)
1. a
2. Possible answer includes, "Why did the mother choose that piece of fruit?"

Week 7: Day 4 (page 47)
1. d
2. Possible answer includes, "Watch the chimps."

Week 7: Day 5 (page 48)
Drawings will vary.
1. Possible answer includes, "It helps the young chimpanzee learn the skills it needs as an adult."

Week 8: Day 1 (page 49)
1. a
2. c

Week 8: Day 2 (page 50)
1. d
2. d

Week 8: Day 3 (page 51)
1. a
2. Possible answer includes, "What does the polar bear mother teach her cub?"

Week 8: Day 4 (page 52)
1. a
2. Possible answer includes, "Encourage the cub to hunt."

Week 8: Day 5 (page 53)
1. Possible answer includes, "To learn."
2. Drawings will vary.

Week 9: Day 1 (page 54)
1. b
2. a

Week 9: Day 2 (page 55)
1. c
2. a

Week 9: Day 3 (page 56)
1. a
2. Possible answer includes, "Why are the adult's feathers pink?"

Week 9: Day 4 (page 57)
1. c
2. Possible answers include, "Ask the zookeeper," or "Look it up."

Week 9: Day 5 (page 58)
cub matches with bear
pinky matches with mouse
fawn matches with deer
calf matches with bull
chick matches with rooster
kitten matches with cat

Answer Key *(cont.)*

Week 10: Day 1 (page 59)
1. c
2. b

Week 10: Day 2 (page 60)
1. a
2. b

Week 10: Day 3 (page 61)
1. c
2. Possible answer includes, "How are these plants the same and different from the adult plants?"

Week 10: Day 4 (page 62)
1. b
2. Possible answers include, "Leaf shape," "Leaf size," "Size of the plant," and "Number of tomatoes."

Week 10: Day 5 (page 63)
Students should circle fruit, runner, and flowers.
1. Fruit and runner.

Week 11: Day 1 (page 64)
1. d
2. a

Week 11: Day 2 (page 65)
1. c
2. b

Week 11: Day 3 (page 66)
1. c
2. Possible answer includes, "Why does the dog have amber eyes?"

Week 11: Day 4 (page 67)
1. a
2. Possible answer includes, "The color of its fur."

Week 11: Day 5 (page 68)
Drawings will vary.

Week 12: Day 1 (page 69)
1. a
2. a

Week 12: Day 2 (page 70)
1. b
2. a

Week 12: Day 3 (page 71)
1. d
2. Possible answer includes, "Does the type of food each twin eats affect how they look?"

Week 12: Day 4 (page 72)
1. a
2. Possible answer includes, "Compare my traits to family members' traits."

Week 12: Day 5 (page 73)
Drawings will vary.

Physical Science

Week 1: Day 1 (page 74)
1. c
2. d

Week 1: Day 2 (page 75)
1. c
2. c

Week 1: Day 3 (page 76)
1. a
2. Possible answer includes, "Why does each instrument make a different sound?"

Week 1: Day 4 (page 77)
1. a
2. Possible answer includes, "Maria can make her own instruments and take notes about the sounds each one makes."

Week 1: Day 5 (page 78)
The rubber bands, the bottom of the pot, and the round ends of the spoons should be circled.

Week 2: Day 1 (page 79)
1. d
2. a

Week 2: Day 2 (page 80)
1. b
2. d

Week 2: Day 3 (page 81)
1. b
2. Possible answers include, "Why does the frog's throat inflate?" and "Why doesn't the frog open its mouth when it croaks?"

Week 2: Day 4 (page 82)
1. c
2. Possible answer includes, "She can put her hand on her throat when she talks."

Answer Key (cont.)

Week 2: Day 5 (page 83)

rattlesnake mouth: hiss; rattlesnake tail: rattle
cat mouth: meow; cat throat: purr
frog throat: croak

Week 3: Day 1 (page 84)

1. b
2. c

Week 3: Day 2 (page 85)

1. c
2. b

Week 3: Day 3 (page 86)

1. b
2. Possible answer includes, "Why do the earmuffs make it hard to hear?"

Week 3: Day 4 (page 87)

1. a
2. Possible answer includes, "Luis can turn it loud and see how far away he can hear it."

Week 3: Day 5 (page 88)

near music: 5
far from music: 1
wearing earmuffs: 4
underwater: 3

Week 4: Day 1 (page 89)

1. c
2. a

Week 4: Day 2 (page 90)

1. b
2. c

Week 4: Day 3 (page 91)

1. b
2. Possible answer includes, "How do light bulbs work?"

Week 4: Day 4 (page 92)

1. a
2. Possible answer includes, "A night light because it will light up more of the room."

Week 4: Day 5 (page 93)

Students should circle candle flames, street lamp, fireworks, sun, headlights, and camp fire.

Week 5: Day 1 (page 94)

1. b
2. c

Week 5: Day 2 (page 95)

1. c
2. a

Week 5: Day 3 (page 96)

1. b
2. Possible answer includes, "How do fireflies light up?"

Week 5: Day 4 (page 97)

1. b
2. Possible answer includes, "Bring several different light sources outside, and test them one at a time."

Week 5: Day 5 (page 98)

1. Possible answers include, "Lamp," "The sun," or any of the other items that the student drew.

Week 6: Day 1 (page 99)

1. d
2. a

Week 6: Day 2 (page 100)

1. b
2. a

Week 6: Day 3 (page 101)

1. b
2. Possible answer includes, "How can I make invisible ink?"

Week 6: Day 4 (page 102)

1. a
2. Possible answer includes, "An envelope because you can't see through it."

Week 6: Day 5 (page 103)

Students should circle the lemon, water, and hair dryer.

1. Possible answer includes, "When I'm trying to send a message to my friend that is a secret."

Week 7: Day 1 (page 104)

1. b
2. a

Week 7: Day 2 (page 105)

1. d
2. a

Week 7: Day 3 (page 106)

1. b
2. Possible answer includes, "What do different types of material do to a beam of light?"

Answer Key (cont.)

Week 7: Day 4 (page 107)
1. d
2. Possible answer includes, "Find opaque, transparent and translucent materials, and shine the light on them."

Week 7: Day 5 (page 108)
apple: opaque
window: transparent
tissue paper: translucent
clear plastic bottle: transparent

Week 8: Day 1 (page 109)
1. a
2. b

Week 8: Day 2 (page 110)
1. a
2. d

Week 8: Day 3 (page 111)
1. b
2. Possible answer includes, "Why does light bounce off a mirror?"

Week 8: Day 4 (page 112)
1. c
2. Possible answer includes, "He can experiment with shining the light on different things."

Week 8: Day 5 (page 113)
Labels from top to bottom: light, wall, flashlight
Possible answer includes: "The light bounces off."

Week 9: Day 1 (page 114)
1. c
2. d

Week 9: Day 2 (page 115)
1. a
2. b

Week 9: Day 3 (page 116)
1. b
2. Possible answer includes, "How can we make our cheers louder for everyone to hear?"

Week 9: Day 4 (page 117)
1. d
2. Possible answers include, "They can use megaphones," or "They can cheer louder."

Week 9: Day 5 (page 118)
Examples of drawings are elevators, fire trucks, police cars, ambulances, and fire alarms.
1. Possible answers include, "It makes sure blind people can hear the message," or, "It makes sure deaf people can see the message."

Week 10: Day 1 (page 119)
1. d
2. d

Week 10: Day 2 (page 120)
1. a
2. a
3. Answers will vary. Examples include, "cat," "dog," and "fun" in Morse Code.

Week 10: Day 3 (page 121)
1. b
2. Possible answer includes, "What is the best way to communicate with my friend once she moves?"

Week 10: Day 4 (page 122)
1. c
2. Possible answer includes, "He could use video chat to talk to his friend."

Week 10: Day 5 (page 123)
megaphone: Far Away
headphones: Close By
walkie talkie: Far Away
1 Answers will vary.

Week 11: Day 1 (page 124)
1. a
2. c

Week 11: Day 2 (page 125)
1. b
2. a

Week 11: Day 3 (page 126)
1. d
2. Possible answer includes, "How can I use the drum to send a message?"

Week 11: Day 4 (page 127)
1. c
2. Possible answer includes, "Make a pattern of drum beats and assign it a meaning."

Week 11: Day 5 (page 128)
Drawings will vary.
1. Possible answer includes, "A loud drum so more people can hear it."

Answer Key *(cont.)*

Week 12: Day 1 (page 129)
1. c
2. a

Week 12: Day 2 (page 130)
1. b
2. a

Week 12: Day 3 (page 131)
1. a
2. Possible answer includes, "How do spotlights work?"

Week 12: Day 4 (page 132)
1. a
2. Possible answer includes, "Shine a light on things on the floor."

Week 12: Day 5 (page 133)
Drawings will vary.
1. Answers will vary.

Earth and Space Science

Week 1: Day 1 (page 134)
1. c
2. a

Week 1: Day 2 (page 135)
1. b
2. a

Week 1: Day 3 (page 136)
1. a
2. Possible answer includes, "Why does the sun move across the sky?

Week 1: Day 4 (page 137)
1. c
2. Possible answer includes, "He can take notes of how the sun moves and look for patterns."

Week 1: Day 5 (page 138)
West: 8:00 p.m.
Middle: 12:00 p.m.
East: 6:00 a.m.
1. Possible answer includes, "In the eastern part."

Week 2: Day 1 (page 139)
1. b
2. c

Week 2: Day 2 (page 140)
1. d
2. a

Week 2: Day 3 (page 141)
1. a
2. Possible answer includes, "Why does the moon look like it changes shape?"

Week 2: Day 4 (page 142)
1. a
2. Possible answer includes, "Look at the moon every day, and draw what it looks like."

Week 2: Day 5 (page 143)
January 18 Sunrise: 7:30 a.m.
January 19 Sunset: 5:47 p.m.
1. 7:27 a.m. because the time goes down by one minute every day.

Week 3: Day 1 (page 144)
1. b
2. a

Week 3: Day 2 (page 145)
1. c
2. a

Week 3: Day 3 (page 146)
1. a
2. Possible answers include, "Why is the sun moving?" or "Will it keep moving the same way every day?"

Week 3: Day 4 (page 147)
1. a
2. Possible answer includes, "Look at the sun at the same time every day for a week. Take note of where it is each day."

Week 3: Day 5 (page 148)
Morning: Sun drawn above tree in the East
Noon: Sun drawn above house in the middle
Afternoon: Sun drawn above bush in the West

Week 4: Day 1 (page 149)
1. b
2. a

Week 4: Day 2 (page 150)
1. c
2. a

Week 4: Day 3 (page 151)
1. a
2. Possible answer includes, "Does the amount of daylight stay the same all year?"

Answer Key (cont.)

Week 4: Day 4 (page 152)
1. a
2. Possible answer includes, "Write down the sunrise and sunset times every month."

Week 4: Day 5 (page 153)
9: winter
14: summer
8: winter
13: summer
1. winter

Week 5: Day 1 (page 154)
1. a
2. d

Week 5: Day 2 (page 155)
1. b
2. c

Week 5: Day 3 (page 156)
1. c
2. Possible answer includes, "Does the sun follow the same path every day?"

Week 5: Day 4 (page 157)
1. a
2. Possible answer includes, "He can track the shadows and see how they change with the time of day."

Week 5: Day 5 (page 158)
Morning matches with middle image (Sun in East)
Noon matches with top image (Sun above tree)
Afternoon matches bottom image (Sun in West)
1. Yes, because it is in certain parts of the sky at certain times of day.

Week 6: Day 1 (page 159)
1. a
2. a

Week 6: Day 2 (page 160)
1. d
2. a

Week 6: Day 3 (page 161)
1. a
2. Possible answer includes, "Does it follow the same path every day?"

Week 6: Day 4 (page 162)
1. a
2. Possible answer includes, "Track when the moon rises for a few days, and look for a pattern."

Week 6: Day 5 (page 163)
Drawings will vary and should look like one of the moon phases.

Week 7: Day 1 (page 164)
1. a
2. d

Week 7: Day 2 (page 165)
1. a
2. a

Week 7: Day 3 (page 166)
1. d
2. Possible answers include, "What are the different moon phases called?" or "What moon phase will come next?"

Week 7: Day 4 (page 167)
1. a
2. Possible answer includes, "Draw the moon shape over the month and look for a pattern."

Week 7: Day 5 (page 168)
1. Possible answer includes, "In a full moon, you can see the whole thing. In a new moon, the moon looks dark."
2. Possible answer includes, "It gets smaller and then bigger."

Week 8: Day 1 (page 169)
1. d
2. a

Week 8: Day 2 (page 170)
1. b
2. b

Week 8: Day 3 (page 171)
1. b
2. Possible answer includes, "Why is it gray and cratered?"

Week 8: Day 4 (page 172)
1. a
2. Possible answer includes, "Read a book about the moon."

Answer Key (cont.)

Week 8: Day 5 (page 173)

Possible answer:

Moon: craters

Earth: water, land

1. Possible answer includes, "The Earth has everything that it needs to support life. The moon cannot support life."
2. Possible answer includes, "Because there is no air."

Week 9: Day 1 (page 174)

1. a
2. a

Week 9: Day 2 (page 175)

1. c
2. a

Week 9: Day 3 (page 176)

1. c
2. Possible answer includes, "Why do the stars look like they move?"

Week 9: Day 4 (page 177)

1. a
2. Possible answer includes, "Take notes on where different constellations are each night."

Week 9: Day 5 (page 178)

Answers will vary. Students should draw a night sky that includes a variety of stars.

Week 10: Day 1 (page 179)

1. c
2. d

Week 10: Day 2 (page 180)

1. a
2. c

Week 10: Day 3 (page 181)

1. a
2. Possible answer includes, "How bright are they compared to the sun?"

Week 10: Day 4 (page 182)

1. b
2. Possible answer includes, "Shine a flashlight on the ceiling to represent a star, and turn a lamp on to represent the sun."

Week 10: Day 5 (page 183)

1. Answers will vary.
2. bright

Week 11: Day 1 (page 184)

1. d
2. b

Week 11: Day 2 (page 185)

1. a
2. c

Week 11: Day 3 (page 186)

1. b
2. Possible answer includes, "Why do the stars look grouped together?"

Week 11: Day 4 (page 187)

1. a
2. Possible answer includes, "Fran can check out a book from the library."

Week 11: Day 5 (page 188)

Answers will vary. Students should draw at least three stars and name them.

1. Possible answer includes, "Because it is my name."

Week 12: Day 1 (page 189)

1. b
2. d

Week 12: Day 2 (page 190)

1. b
2. a

Week 12: Day 3 (page 191)

1. b
2. Possible answer includes, "What makes the stars twinkle?"

Week 12: Day 4 (page 192)

1. d
2. Possible answer includes, "Use a light with a dimmer switch, and switch between dim and bright."

Week 12: Day 5 (page 193)

1. Possible answer includes, "Because they are blocked by clouds."
2. Yes

Student Name: _____ Date: _____

Developing Questions Rubric

Directions: Complete this rubric every four weeks to evaluate students' Day 3 activity sheets. Only one rubric is needed per student. Their work over the four weeks can be evaluated together. Evaluate their work in each category by writing a score in each row. Then, add up their scores, and write the total on the line. Students may earn up to 5 points in each row and up to 15 points total.

Skill	5	3	1	Score
Asking Scientific Questions	Asks scientific questions related to text all or nearly all the time.	Asks scientific questions related to text most of the time.	Does not ask scientific questions related to text.	
Interpreting Text	Correctly interprets texts to answer questions all or nearly all the time.	Correctly interprets texts to answer questions most of the time.	Does not correctly interpret texts to answer questions.	
Applying Information	Applies new information to form questions all or nearly all the time.	Applies new information to form questions most of the time.	Does not apply new information to form questions.	

Total Points: _____

51407—180 Days of Science

Student Name: _____ Date: _____

Planning Solutions Rubric

Directions: Complete this rubric every four weeks to evaluate students' Day 4 activity sheets. Only one rubric is needed per student. Their work over the four weeks can be evaluated together. Evaluate their work in each category by writing a score in each row. Then, add up their scores, and write the total on the line. Students may earn up to 5 points in each row and up to 15 points total.

Skill	5	3	1	Score
Making Predictions	Plans reasonable tests to study topics all or nearly all the time.	Plans reasonable tests to study topics most of the time.	Does not plan reasonable tests to study topics.	
Choosing Next Steps	Makes reasonable predictions all or nearly all the time.	Makes reasonable predictions most of the time.	Does not make reasonable predictions.	
Choosing Next Steps	Chooses reasonable next steps for tests all or nearly all the time.	Chooses reasonable next steps for tests most of the time.	Does not choose reasonable next steps for tests.	

Total Points: _____

Student Name: _____ Date: _____

Communicating Results Rubric

Directions: Complete this rubric every four weeks to evaluate students' Day 5 activity sheets. Only one rubric is needed per student. Their work over the four weeks can be evaluated together. Evaluate their work in each category by writing a score in each row. Then, add up their scores, and write the total on the line. Students may earn up to 5 points in each row and up to 15 points total.

Skill	5	3	1	Score
Showing Data	Creates charts and graphs to correctly show data all or nearly all the time.	Creates charts and graphs to correctly show data most of the time.	Does not create charts and graphs to correctly show data.	
Making Connections	Makes connections between new information and prior knowledge all or nearly all the time.	Makes connections between new information and prior knowledge most of the time.	Does not make connections between new information and prior knowledge.	
Explaining Results	Applies new information to form questions all or nearly all the time.	Applies new information to form questions most of the time.	Does not apply new information to form questions.	

Total Points: _____

51407—180 Days of Science

Life Science Analysis Chart

Directions: Record the total of each student's Day 1 and Day 2 scores from the four weeks. Then, record each student's rubric scores (pages 202–204). Add the totals, and record the sums in the Total Scores column. Record the average class score in the last row.

Student Name	Week 4						Week 8						Week 12						Total Scores
	Day 1	Day 2	DQ	PS	CR		Day 1	Day 2	DQ	PS	CR		Day 1	Day 2	DQ	PS	CR		
Average Classroom Score																			

DQ = Developing Questions, PS = Planning Solutions, CR = Communicating Results

Physical Science Analysis Chart

Directions: Record the total of each student's Day 1 and Day 2 scores from the four weeks. Then, record each student's rubric scores (pages 202–204). Add the totals, and record the sums in the Total Scores column. Record the average class score in the last row.

Student Name	Week 4						Week 8						Week 12						Total Scores
	Day 1	Day 2	DQ	PS	CR		Day 1	Day 2	DQ	PS	CR		Day 1	Day 2	DQ	PS	CR		
Average Classroom Score																			

DQ = Developing Questions, PS = Planning Solutions, CR = Communicating Results

Earth and Space Science Analysis Chart

Directions: Record the total of each student's Day 1 and Day 2 scores from the four weeks. Then, record each student's rubric scores (pages 202–204). Add the totals, and record the sums in the Total Scores column. Record the average class score in the last row.

Student Name	Week 4						Week 8						Week 12						Total Scores
	Day 1	Day 2	DQ	PS	CR		Day 1	Day 2	DQ	PS	CR		Day 1	Day 2	DQ	PS	CR		
Average Classroom Score																			

DQ = Developing Questions, PS = Planning Solutions, CR = Communicating Results

Digital Resources

To access digital resources, go to this website and enter the following code: 17757820
www.teachercreatedmaterials.com/administrators/download-files/

Rubrics

Resource	Filename
Developing Questions Rubric	questionsrubric.pdf
Planning Solutions Rubric	solutionsrubric.pdf
Communicating Results Rubric	resultsrubric.pdf

Item Analysis Sheets

Resource	Filename
Life Science Analysis Chart	LSanalysischart.pdf
	LSanalysischart.docx
	LSanalysischart.xlsx
Physical Science Analysis Chart	PSanalysischart.pdf
	PSanalysischart.docx
	PSanalysischart.xlsx
Earth and Space Science Analysis Chart	ESSanalysischart.pdf
	ESSanalysischart.docx
	ESSanalysischart.xlsx

Standards

Resource	Filename
Standards Charts	standards.pdf